The First
America's Team

★★★ *The First* ★★★
AMERICA'S TEAM
the 1962
GREEN BAY PACKERS

BY BOB BERGHAUS

Foreword by Bart Starr

CLERISY PRESS

The First America's Team: The 1962 Green Bay Packers

For further information, contact the publisher:
Clerisy Press
P.O. Box 8874
Cincinnati, OH 45208-0874
clerisypress.com

Library of Congress Cataloging-in-Publication Data

Berghaus, Bob, 1954–
    The first America's team : the 1962 Green Bay Packers / by Bob
        Berghaus. — 1st ed.
    p. cm.
    ISBN-13: 978-1-57860-442-5 (pbk.)
    ISBN-10: 1-57860-442-7 ()
    1. Green Bay Packers (Football team)—History. I. Title.
    GV956.G7B46 2011
    796.332'640977561—dc23
                                        2011022283

Distributed by Publishers Group West
Edited by Jack Heffron
Cover designed by Scott McGrew
Interior designed by Annie Long
All photos courtesy of the *Green Bay Press-Gazette*
First edition, first printing

Thank you, Lisa.

As with most accomplishments in my life, I wouldn't have been able to complete this book without the support of my wife, Lisa. She's a loving mother and wife whose honesty and humor spurs me on more than she realizes. I don't know where I would be without her.

table *of* contents

Foreword

by Bart Starr

Entering 1962, we expected to have a very good season because we were coming off a truly special one in 1961. We finished it off in as great a way as you could close out a season when we beat a strong Giants team 37–0 to win our first National Football League championship under coach Vince Lombardi.

We had exceptional talent in 1962. Nine of my teammates were eventually elected to the Pro Football Hall of Fame and there are several others who should be in as well. Obviously, we had the leadership of Coach Lombardi, who gave us a sense of direction as soon as he arrived in 1959.

We started the 1962 season very strong, winning our first three games by fairly sizeable margins. We had that close call with the Lions in the fourth game, when Herb Adderley intercepted a pass in the final minute that set up a short field goal for Paul Hornung, enabling us to win the game.

We kept winning, and at some point reporters began asking us about the possibility of an unbeaten season. I can tell you that wasn't our focus, that I don't think any one of us thought in those terms because of the leadership and direction by Coach Lombardi. What we were thinking about was just going at it game by game, week by week, and just seeing where that would take us.

Under the direction of Coach Lombardi we won our first ten games before we finally lost to the Lions in Detroit in the annual Thanksgiving Day game. Obviously when you have that kind of pressure building and you suffer a loss, it can be very damaging to you and very disappointing. But I think because of Coach Lombardi's leadership we were able to keep a very narrowly focused direction in front of us. Somehow, you just work your way through those things, something we were able to do.

We won our last three games to set up another championship game with the Giants. This one was played in Yankee Stadium, and the Giants were ready for us because of what had happened the previous year. I don't think we looked at it as pressure. We were more concerned about the quality of team we were facing. We had a lot of respect for the Giants, but I think the focus was that this is going to be a game on the road in front of a hostile crowd.

The Giants were a formidable foe, no question about that. They had a 12–2 record, at one point winning nine straight games. They had excellent leadership, a very good defense, and of course they had quarterback Y.A. Tittle, who had an outstanding year.

The strength of our team was on display in that ball game because it was one of the coldest games at that time, and it was very, very windy. I'll always remember how cold and windy it was because I had never seen the sideline benches be blown over. They actually blew over and onto the field during the game. It was quite a sight.

Because we had a strong running game we were able to win that ball game. I didn't have the arm strength and accuracy to deal with those conditions, so I was grateful we had the strength of the running game because I could lean on that throughout the game. Because the Giants focused on stopping our running attack, it helped when we did have to throw.

That was the second of our five championships under Coach Lombardi. We went on to win three more with him, something I'm proud of to this day. Coach Lombardi meant the world to me. I appreciate the confidence he showed in me on the football field, and I'm grateful for how he helped me away from the field.

One thing that was characteristic of him was the pursuit of excellence. He said the pursuit of excellence would make you a better person than you otherwise might be content to be. I know I'm a better person than I otherwise would have been because of the time I was able to spend with the man.

CHAPTER 1

Football as It Should Be Played

"Football is two things. It's blocking and tackling. You block and tackle better than the team you're playing, you win."

That was the mindset of Vince Lombardi, who in 1962 was the most famous football coach of what was probably the most revered professional football team in America. During that season, his Green Bay Packers blocked and tackled better than the other thirteen teams in the National Football League. They led the league in scoring with 415 points, and the 148 points given up by Green Bay's hard-hitting defense was the fewest in the league.

Those totals, by the way, were also better than all eight teams in the rival American Football League, which was in its third year of existence. The Packers' winning margin of 19.1 per game was more than 10 points better than all other team in the NFL.

Four years earlier, the Packers were at rock bottom following a 1–10–1 record. Ray "Scooter" McLean, a nice man who didn't understand the meaning of discipline, quit before he would have been dismissed as coach. In the winter of 1959 the Packers hired Lombardi, who had been offensive coordinator for the New York Giants since 1954.

Lombardi was a tough-as-nails guard at Fordham, playing on the legendary "Seven Blocks of Granite" offensive line. After college he became a high school teacher and coach. He returned to Fordham to coach the freshman football team, and then moved on to West Point as an assistant to the legendary Red Blaik. With the Giants, Lombardi became known in NFL circles as a top-flight coordinator, but when head coaching jobs came up he was passed over until he finally got his chance with the Packers at age forty-five.

The Packers won their first three games under Lombardi before losing five in a row to end any hopes of a dramatic worst-to-first turnaround. Struggling at 3–5, the Packers seemed destined to have another losing season. Remarkably, they turned around during the last third of the season, winning their final four games for a 7–5 record and their first winning season in twelve years.

During those four games the Packers outscored their opponents 119–51, scoring almost as many points as the 129 totaled during the first eight games. The defense, by giving up an average of just under 13 points in those final four games, also showed remarkable improvement after allowing an average of 31.8 points per game during the losing streak.

The Packers entered 1960 with thoughts of achieving more than a winning record. They had talent up and down the roster with most of the starters in their mid-twenties. Green Bay won all five of its exhibition games and appeared to have momentum going into the season opener against the Chicago Bears.

Instead, they lost at home to the team coached by legendary George Halas, but then reeled off four straight wins, putting themselves in position to unseat the Baltimore Colts, who had won the last two NFL titles, as champions of the Western Division.

That goal wasn't going to come easily. The Packers won just once during their next four games, falling to 5–4 following a 23–10 loss to the Lions in the traditional Thanksgiving Day game in Detroit, when the Packers looked flat on offense, totaling just 181 yards.

The fortunes of the Green Bay Packers changed dramatically when
Vince Lombardi took the head-coaching job.

They were still in the title race but likely needed to sweep the final three
games. Ten days after the loss to Detroit they traveled to Chicago for a rematch
with the Bears and beat their archrivals by 28 points, setting up a first-place
showdown with the San Francisco 49ers, who, like Green Bay, had a 6–4 record.
The Colts also were 6–4, but that day they dropped a game back after losing
to the Rams. In San Francisco, the Packers defense pitched a shutout, fullback
Jim Taylor rushed for 161 yards, and halfback Paul Hornung provided all the
scoring in a 13–0 win.

The following week the Packers closed out the season with a 35–21 win in
Los Angeles against the Rams. Quarterback Bart Starr completed touchdown
passes of 91 yards to Boyd Dowler and 57 yards to Max McGee. The win put the
Packers in the championship game for the first time since 1944.

They faced the Philadelphia Eagles, trying to win their first title since 1949.
The Packers had a 13–10 lead early in the fourth quarter but a long kickoff return

by Ted Dean set up a winning touchdown, and the Packers lost 17–13. After that defeat, Lombardi told his players they'd never lose another championship game.

The title game appearance in 1960 wasn't a fluke. The next year, Green Bay cruised to the Western Conference title and hosted the Giants in the 1961 championship game at City Stadium. Lombardi was fond of the Mara family, which owned the Giants. He had attended Fordham University with Wellington, the son of Tim, who founded the Giants in 1925.

When it came time for the game on December 31, Lombardi forgot about friendship for an afternoon. After a scoreless first quarter, his Packers blocked and tackled considerably better than the big-city team, scoring 24 points in the second quarter on the way to a 37–0 victory. It could have been worse—much worse.

"I was mad at Vince," Paul Hornung said years later. "We could have scored 70 against them but he pulled the starters out early. He liked the Maras and didn't want to rub it in. We had a tremendous team and we played a tremendous game." Hornung had scored 19 points in the game by himself.

Football was much different in the 1960s than it is today, when people all over the country have television access to every game that is played. With rare exceptions, there were only three NFL games televised nationally during a season: the championship game; the Thanksgiving Day game in Detroit; and the exhibition game between the reigning NFL champions and college all-stars. Nevertheless, despite the lack of TV exposure nationwide, America was getting to know the Green Bay Packers.

Lombardi was receiving mail from throughout the country from people who started Packer fan clubs. People were finding out about the team from the little town through newspaper and magazine stories.

Hornung and Taylor were piling up yards on Lombardi's famed Power Sweep, which was making his offensive line famous, especially the guards. Center Jim Ringo, guards Fuzzy Thurston and Jerry Kramer, and tackles Forrest Gregg and Bob Skoronski, who alternated at left tackle with Norm Masters, formed a unit that was second to none. The defense was led by linemen Willie Davis and Henry Jordan. Middle linebacker Ray Nitschke was beginning to make a name for himself as were Willie Wood and Herb Adderley, who made the Packers' secondary one to fear for opposing quarterbacks.

And of course there was Starr, a seventeenth-round draft pick out of the University of Alabama in 1956. He was in charge of Lombardi's offense. All of the above, with the exception of Kramer, Thurston, Masters, and Skoronski, would wind up in the Pro Football Hall of Fame.

"Think of the names that were playing up there," said Tom Matte, a former halfback for the Baltimore Colts. "It was just a fantastic time for football. The Orioles were a good baseball team but Baltimore was a football town. Green Bay was a good football town, the Cleveland Browns at the time, and the New York Giants, played in good football towns.

"Look what the Baltimore Colts and the New York Giants did for football in 1958 and '59. Then Lombardi came to Green Bay. It was a time when people were looking for a national sport. Baseball had always been that, but to be honest with you, baseball fans are just not as enthusiastic as football fans. They're just crazy. They love the game; they love the contact."

The Packers were loved throughout Wisconsin. They played part of their home schedule in Milwaukee, one hundred miles to the south, halfway between Chicago and Green Bay, which became known as Titletown when the Packers won the 1961 championship.

Milwaukee had the Braves, who had moved to the city from Boston before the 1953 season. While the Packers of the fifties struggled to win, the Braves were popular and set a National League attendance record, drawing 1.8 million fans. They eventually gave Wisconsin baseball fans a winner, beating the New York Yankees in seven games in the 1957 World Series. Led by the home run duo of Hank Aaron and Eddie Mathews, the Braves returned to the Fall Classic the following year but lost game seven to the Yankees in Milwaukee. The Braves and Los Angeles Dodgers tied for the National League title in 1959, but the Dodgers won a playoff and went to the World Series. The Braves started to decline in 1960, and within a few years ownership was looking to relocate the club. The team moved to Atlanta following the 1965 season, leaving Milwaukee without baseball until 1970, when a group led by Bud Selig, then owner of an automobile dealership, bought the Seattle Pilots and made them the Brewers. Years later Selig would become commissioner of Major League Baseball.

County Stadium, the home of the Braves, also was a part-time home for the Packers, who began playing at least one game a year in Milwaukee beginning in 1953. When the baseball park was built, the Packers played two games a season there through 1960. When the NFL expanded from a twelve- to a fourteen-game schedule in 1961, Milwaukee picked up another home game.

Green Bay fans didn't like sharing their team, but by 1962, the Milwaukee stadium could pack in over 46,000 fans, 7,000 more than Green Bay's City Stadium held. Playing in Milwaukee was good for business, and it also helped the team create a bond with the entire state.

The Packers' success from 1961 carried over into 1962 as they swept through six exhibition games and the first ten games of the regular season. Writers from the big newspapers and magazines continued to travel to Green Bay to tell their readers about the magic that was happening in the little town of 63,000 people. Before the 1962 title game, *Time* magazine put Lombardi on its cover, which proclaimed football "The sport of the '60s." The story referred to Lombardi as "the world's greatest football coach." His sport was overtaking baseball as the national pastime, and Lombardi's Packers had become the face of the NFL.

During those first ten games in 1962, Lombardi's men scored 34 or more points in six of those contests and recorded three shutouts. Their ninth win was a 49–0 whitewash of the Philadelphia Eagles, the team that had beaten them in the 1960 NFL championship game 17–13. The Packers had 37 first downs while setting a team record with 628 yards and holding the Eagles to 3 first downs and 54 yards.

The Packers finally suffered a loss when the Detroit Lions sacked Starr eleven times during a 26–14 win in the annual Thanksgiving Day game in Detroit. But they came back and won their final three games, although they struggled on the West Coast swing. They trailed the San Francisco 49ers 21–10 at Kezar Stadium before rallying with 21 second-half points for a 31–21 win. The following week at the Los Angeles Coliseum, they were pushed to the brink by the one-win Rams before escaping with a 20–17 triumph to complete the thirteen-win regular season.

The Packers were not the only football team being talked about in Wisconsin that year. The University of Wisconsin, the state's entry in the Big Ten Conference, also was having a special season. The Badgers won their first four games before losing to Ohio State in Columbus, 14–7. The Badgers bounced back and continued to win. In their seventh game they administered a 37–6 whipping on unbeaten and top-ranked Northwestern, which was coached by Ara Parseghian, who in two years would be coaching at Notre Dame.

The Badgers finished the regular season 8–1 and ranked No. 2 in the country behind Southern Cal. Those teams met in the Rose Bowl and put on a wild show. The Trojans led 42–14 early in the fourth quarter before the Badgers made a furious rally that fell just short, 42–37.

Pat Richter, an All-American tight end for Wisconsin who would go on to have an eight-year NFL career with the Washington Redskins, said there was a strong bond between the Packers and Badgers. Richter, who was from Madison and also played basketball and baseball for Wisconsin, got to know many of the Packers at athletic banquets during and after that season because he shared the dais with them. In that classic game against Southern California, Richter set a Rose Bowl record with 11 catches for 163 yards. The Badgers wouldn't return to the Rose Bowl for another thirty-one years, but they did it with the help of Richter, who, as Wisconsin's athletic director, hired Barry Alvarez, a forty-three-year-old assistant coach from Notre Dame. Alvarez would lead the Badgers to three Rose Bowl championships.

"Milt Bruin, our coach, had a good relationship with Lombardi, who reached out to the state, and Milt took it upon himself to go up there and learn as much as he could," said Richter, who played for Lombardi in 1969 during the coach's one season with Washington. "Milt and his staff went to Green Bay and learned their offense. We actually installed the sweep type of offense, which was fairly innovative at that time. They didn't have a big laundry list of plays. It was simple, but what you were taught you had to do well."

The Giants didn't start as fast as the Packers in 1962. They lost their first game in and were 3–2 and in second place in the Eastern Division before hitting their stride. Led by quarterback Y.A. Tittle, the Giants won their final nine games and finished the regular season with a 12–2 record for their fourth division title in five years. They clinched the title in the twelfth week of the season with a 26–24 win over the Chicago Bears.

Tittle directed a pass-first offense that was all about the big play. He threw for 3,224 yards and 33 touchdown passes. His favorite target was split end Del Shofner, who caught 12 touchdown strikes and finished the regular season with 53 balls for 1,133 yards, a staggering 21.4 yards per catch.

Frank Gifford, Lombardi's left halfback when the coach was an assistant with the Giants, was now a flanker. Gifford sustained a serious head injury in 1960 after a violent collision with Eagles linebacker Chuck Bednarik, forcing him to retire for a season. Though not touching the ball nearly as much as he did when he was a ball carrier, Gifford was still productive in the regular season, catching 39 passes, including seven for touchdowns. Like Shofner, when he made a catch it was for big yards, as Gifford averaged 20.2 yards per play. The Giants could be explosive. They scored 398 points, and four times during their final eight games, they torched opposing teams for 41 or more points.

The Giants had last won an NFL title in 1956. They lost to the Colts in the 1958 game, the famous one that went to sudden death, and again to the Colts in 1959. From 1958 through 1962 they were one of the NFL's most consistent teams with an overall record of 47–14–3, but the three bridesmaid finishes gave the team a reputation for not being able to win the truly big game. And the third of those championship losses, in 1961, was just plain embarrassing.

That game was played on a cold, relatively calm day in Green Bay. The temperature was 17 degrees, and the winds blew at ten miles per hour. Tittle struggled to throw, and the Giants squandered two early scoring opportunities before the Packers exploded for 24 points in the second quarter.

"We depended on the forward pass," Tittle said. "We didn't get the good weather, and it hurt us a lot."

In 1962, the Packers were looking to repeat as champions; the Giants were looking to avenge one of the worst losses many players on the team had experienced.

The Packers had two weeks to prepare for the 1962 championship game, which was beneficial because they were a beat-up team. Among those hurting was Jim Ringo, who had a nerve problem in his right arm that caused it to go numb. Ironically, Ringo's injury worsened in practice. In *Nitschke*, a biography of the Packers' middle linebacker, Ray Nitschke said Lombardi pulled him aside leading up to the title game and instructed him to go after the Green Bay offense like it was the Giants' offense. Lombardi was fearful his team lacked intensity leading up to the game, and he thought Nitschke could change that.

One day the middle linebacker hit Ringo so hard that it left the center with a pinched muscle in his neck. The pain ran down to his arm and became a serious problem in the days leading up to the game.

Following a workout at Yankee Stadium two days before the game, Lombardi asked Ringo how he felt. Ringo told the coach he couldn't feel his arm and that he didn't think he'd be able to play.

The exchange was witnessed by Dave Klein, a reporter for the *Newark Star-Ledger*. According to *Nitschke*, Lombardi lost his temper at the reporter for being there. Ringo was more diplomatic, telling Klein that if the Giants knew about his problem they'd go after his arm. He promised the reporter an exclusive interview following the game if he didn't report on the injury. Klein agreed.

Hornung was playing, despite being mostly inactive since injuring his knee in the fifth game. Outside linebacker Dan Currie had missed three games with a bad knee, although he returned for the final game against the Rams.

The week before the game, Lombardi had a sign installed above the door leading to the Packers' locker room: "Home of the GREEN BAY PACKERS 'The Yankees of Football.'"

The sign served as motivation, but it may have also been a psychological move to get the Packers thinking of where the championship game was going to be played. Yankee Stadium was *the* sporting arena of the era. The house that Ruth built; the home of the team that had dominated major league baseball since the 1920s. Yankee Stadium also was the site of several historic college football games between Army and Notre Dame and also home to some of the biggest heavyweight title fights of all time. In 1927 Jack Dempsey came from behind to beat Jack Sharkey there. In 1936 German Max Schmeling knocked out unbeaten Joe Louis in the twelfth round at Yankee Stadium. They had a

Equipment manager Dad Braisher adjusts a motivational sign in the team's locker room in late December, 1962.

rematch two years later at the same venue, and Louis knocked out the German in the first round to win the title.

The Packers knew they would see a different Giants team than the one they faced in 1961. The Giants were looking for payback—and to prove that the 37-point loss the previous year was a fluke.

"We were concerned about the quality of team we were facing and playing on the road in '62; that's where the focus was," said Bart Starr, who had his best season, completing 62.5 percent of his passes while directing the most potent offense in the game. "We had a lot of respect for the Giants, but I think the focus was more that it was a road game, in New York, where we would be facing a hostile crowd, so to speak. We also recognized the strength that the Giants had that year. They had excellent leadership, and Tittle was a very strong and talented quarterback."

Still seething from the 37-point humiliation the year before, the Giants wanted the Packers to leave Yankee Stadium the way they had left Green Bay twelve months earlier.

"I've never been as anxious to play a game as this one," Giants defensive end Andy Robustelli said at the time "We will absolutely kill the bastards. It's the only way I'll be able to forget about the one out there last year. It won't be enough to just win the game. We have to destroy the Packers and Lombardi. It's the only way we can atone for what happened to us last year."

Lombardi knew there would be a sense of awe for many of his players to play such a prestigious game at Yankee Stadium. They had played at the cavernous facility in 1959, but it was a midseason game. This one was different: the Packers were going for their second straight title, and the entire nation would be watching.

The game had special meaning to Jerry Kramer, the Packers talented right guard. He broke his leg midway through the 1961 campaign and missed the championship game. He'd been on the sidelines in Green Bay and had celebrated with his teammates, but it was not the same. He worked hard during the offseason and had a terrific 1962 season, earning consensus All-Pro honors for the first time in his career.

The rematch with the Giants also carried added significance for Kramer because he had become the team's kicker for extra points and field goals when Hornung injured his knee before the midway mark of the '62 season.

"When we got to the game my main concern was not letting the team down, trying to make the field goals, trying to grab a hold of my composure," Kramer recalled in late 2010. "We were in Yankee Stadium and I was about to wet my pants.

"Yankee Stadium was hallowed ground, and it was an awesome experience to walk into the stands, especially for me. With Hornung injured and me kicking out there, it was a pretty damn exciting time for me."

The Packers were a running team, led by Taylor, the powerful fullback who during the season averaged 105 yards per game and scored 19 touchdowns, numbers that helped to beat out Tittle for the league's Most Valuable Player Award. Even though the ground attack was the strength of his offense, Lombardi, after studying hours and hours of film on the Giants, was convinced Starr could beat them through the air. The game plan revolved around the pass, and many expected the championship game to be a wide-open contest between the league's two highest-scoring teams.

The Packers led the NFL that season in eleven offensive categories, including scoring and rushing. The Giants, who scored 391 points, topped the NFL in total offense as they gained more than 5,000 net yards and had a league-leading 35 touchdown passes.

The game also featured many of the game's greatest players, including fifteen that would land in the Hall of Fame. For the Giants: Roosevelt Brown, Frank Gifford, Sam Huff, Robustelli, and Tittle. The Canton-bound Packers were Herb Adderley, Willie Davis, Forrest Gregg, Paul Hornung, Henry Jordan, Ray Nitschke, Jim Ringo, Bart Starr, Jim Taylor, and Willie Wood. In addition, Giants' owner Mara and Packers' coach Lombardi would be voted into the Hall.

For all of these reasons and more, there was great national interest in this championship game. Pro football had been growing in popularity since the 1958 sudden-death championship game between Baltimore and the Giants. This rematch featuring the hard-hitting team from the NFL's smallest market against the big city New Yorkers was going to be a treat for football fans throughout the country.

According to a story in the *Press-Gazette*, players on the winning teams would receive approximately $6,000; losing players would earn $4,000. Both amounts were records. The NFL would earn $632,000 from television, radio, and film rights, a considerable difference from the $75,000 the league made in 1951, the first time a championship game was nationally televised.

———

Game day came and any expectations of a shootout were blown away by a strong wind that swept throughout Yankee Stadium. Gusts ranging from thirty to forty miles per hour made for horrific conditions, especially with the temperature hovering around twenty degrees.

The Packers were ready. As the bus that carried the team and media members arrived at its destination, Nitschke leaped out of his seat and yelled, "Welcome to Yankee Stadium, home of the World Champion Packers."

Defensive end Willie Davis recalled the field feeling like a "parking lot." The grass was gone, and the dirt was frozen. Those who took the field had never remembered conditions being so primitive. At the time it was the coldest many players had felt on a football field. Some of those same players, who five years later beat Dallas in the infamous "Ice Bowl" when the temperature was minus thirteen degrees, recalled Giants Stadium feeling just as cold because of the wind.

"Vince (Lombardi) Jr. once told me he thought it was colder or worse than the Ice Bowl," Kramer said later. "I remember the wind blowing like a bitch. We came out at halftime and our players' bench—it was a small bench without a back on it, just two sides and the setting surface—the wind had blown the bench back onto the playing field. It may have blown maybe ten yards out onto the field. Our capes and all kinds of shit was being strung all over hell and back. The trainers were trying to pick everything up because of that wind. I don't know what the wind chill factor was but it was bitter cold."

The wind was so severe that it tore the American flag that flew in the stadium. One of the cameras used for the national telecast blew over. In the baseball dugouts, photographers built little bonfires to thaw out their cameras. Before the Packers kicked off to begin the game, the ball fell off the tee three times because of heavy wind gusts.

Despite the elements, the Giants fans were ready for the Packers. Shouts of "Beat Green Bay. Beat Green Bay" filled the stadium from the more than 62,000 that attended.

Fans in a team's home market could not watch their team's regular season and playoff games on television because of the NFL's blackout policy, which was in place to protect gate receipts. Because of that policy, many residents of New York City piled into cars and traveled to hotels in Connecticut, New Jersey, and Pennsylvania so they could watch the game on TV.

The primitive conditions forced Lombardi to scrap his plan on surprising the Giants with a passing attack. As usual, the Packers offense would revolve around Taylor, whose every move was being followed by Sam Huff, the Giants All-Pro linebacker. Huff had help; the Giants couldn't wait to hit Taylor over and over.

"They beat the shit out of Taylor," Hornung remembered almost fifty years later.

Early in the game Taylor bit his tongue when he was tackled, causing him to swallow blood for much of the game. He also suffered a cut on his arm and was stitched up by team doctors at halftime. As his teammates tried to thaw out at halftime they heard Taylor scream in agony from the trainer's room while he was being sewn up.

Despite the pain and physical punishment he was enduring, Taylor played like a champion. Of the Packers' forty-six running plays, Taylor was given the ball thirty-one times, finishing with 85 of the toughest yards he would ever gain in a game. During the second quarter with his team up 3–0, thanks to a 26-yard first-quarter field goal by Kramer, Taylor scored the game's only offensive touchdown on a 7-yard run that gave his team a 10–0 lead.

Years later Huff said, "Did everything I could to that sonofabitch."

It turned out that Taylor was playing sick; he was diagnosed with hepatitis a week later.

Davis remembers Taylor being upset because he was considered second fiddle to the great Jim Brown, the Cleveland Browns fullback who led the league in rushing every year he played during his nine-year career—except in 1962, when Taylor won the title with 1,474 yards.

"He was always mindful of Jim Brown," Davis said. "Nothing would have pleased Jim Taylor more than having a breakout game in the championship game so he could say to Jim Brown, 'In your face.'

"The Giants really took it to him that game. He was literally beat up by the end of the game and even into the next week when they discovered he had a sickness. Still he played a tough game and he didn't get one free yard."

Following the game, while talking to reporters, Huff paid the ultimate compliment to the Green Bay fullback.

"Taylor isn't human. No human being could have taken the punishment he got today," Huff said. "Every time he was tackled it was like crashing him down on a cement sidewalk because the ground was as hard as pavement. But he kept bouncing up, snarling at us, and asking for more."

Taylor told reporters that the Giant players taunted him throughout, calling him over-rated.

"I never took a worse beating on a football field," Taylor said. "The Giants hit me hard, and then I hit the ground hard. I got it both ways. I just rammed it right back at them, letting my running do the talking. They couldn't rattle me."

Meanwhile, the Giants offense couldn't get into the end zone. Tittle kept trying to go long, but the gusting winds sometimes pushed the ball several yards back. The Giants had success with short passes but 3 turnovers—1 interception and 2 fumbles—were devastating.

"The ball was like a diving duck," Tittle said after the game. "I threw one pass and it almost came back to me. The short ones worked, but the long ball broke up. We needed the long one."

After the Packers took a 3–0 lead Tittle used short passes to drive to the Packers 15-yard line. Tittle had tight end Joe Walton open on the goal line when he delivered a pass. But Nitschke got his hand on it, tipping it in the air. The ball was intercepted by Dan Currie, who made a long return but staggered as he fell to the ground because his knee gave out. He looked like a punch-drunk fighter trying to stay on his feet before hitting the canvas.

"I go about 30 or 40 yards and it starts to waver and wobble," Currie said after the game. "It's not that strong yet."

The Giants' lone score came in the third quarter, and it was without any help from the offense. Packer flanker Boyd Dowler, who also was the team's punter, had a bad leg, which kept him from punting. That chore fell to Max McGee, who before Dowler arrived had been the punter. He took a snap while standing in his end zone, and Giants defensive back Erich Barnes swooped in untouched and blocked the kick. Giants special team player Jim Collier fell on the ball in the end zone for a touchdown that cut the Packers lead to 10–7.

The crowd at Yankee Stadium was re-energized, and shouts of "Beat Green Bay" rose louder than ever. But Tittle just couldn't deal with the wind. He needed 41 attempts to complete 18 passes for 197 yards. Shofner had 5 receptions for 69 yards but never could get past cornerback Jesse Whittenton, who played much of the game with limited mobility after suffering a jarring hit to the ribs delivered by Giants fullback Phil King. Had it not been so windy, Shofner may have been able to get downfield for an opportunity for a long play.

"I busted up my ribs in the first quarter," Whittenton said after the game. "King had the ball on a sweep or a screen—I don't remember which—and I came up and got it in the side. I had figured to play Del tight, but after that I had to drop off him because I couldn't move around as good as usual. I had to give him the short one, and I'm glad they couldn't throw the long one."

The Packers secondary suffered another loss when safety Willie Wood was ejected in the third quarter after he unintentionally knocked down back judge Tom Kelleher. Wood had tipped a pass directed at Shofner and Kelleher called it interference. Wood approached the official and began to protest when he slipped and hit Kelleher, causing him to fall down. Wood was replaced for the remainder of the game by one-time starter Johnny Symank.

"I was covering Shofner on a crossing pattern," Wood said after the game. "I went for the ball and suddenly I saw the white handkerchief go down. I jumped up to protest and my hand must have hit him in the chest."

Said Kelleher, "In my opinion, Wood committed an overt act in striking me and that called for disqualification. If I had bumped into him it would have been a different matter."

The rest of the scoring was done by Kramer, who during the regular season had made 38 of 39 extra-point attempts and was good on 9 of 11 field-goal tries. He booted a 30-yarder with four minutes left in the third quarter for a 13–7 lead.

Then, with 1:50 remaining in the game, Kramer capped the scoring with a field goal from 29 yards for a 16–7 lead, which on this brutal day was enough to secure a second championship for the team that resided in the NFL's smallest city. As he left the field, Kramer was swamped by his joyous teammates. He had been forced to watch the 37–0 win the previous year because of a broken leg, and now he was a championship game hero.

"If I made that kick, that pretty much meant the game," Kramer said. "So in those situations you try to focus on keeping your head down. That was my focus at that time, keeping my head down and following through. Don't look up prematurely; make sure you hit the ball squarely. I believe I aimed the ball outside the right goal post. The wind was whipping into the post, just circling in the stadium going round and round. When the thing went through I was afraid

Jerry Kramer, who took over kicking duties for the team after the injury to
Paul Hornung, practices his technique during a workout.

I was going to miss it, afraid I was going to be the goat, so it was great relief more
than anything else.

"All the guys were jumping on me. I was feeling like a wide receiver or a
running back for a moment. I never had that kind of reaction before."

Dowler recalled how the big offensive guard swung his foot into the
football.

"He jabbed at the ball," Dowler said. He hit it pretty square, pretty solid, and they went through. It was a pretty good accomplishment when your right guard kicks three field goals in the championship game."

On most days Kramer's point production might have been good enough for him to be selected as the game's MVP by media covering the game. That honor instead went to Nitschke, the bald, ferocious middle linebacker who had tipped the touchdown-bound pass and also had recovered two fumbles.

"The players voted me the game ball, which is an example of what life is like for a lineman in that business," Kramer recalled. "The writers voted Nitschke the game's MVP, and he got the Corvette. I got the game ball, which is a lot more than what most offensive linemen get."

In newspaper accounts of the game, Nitschke seemed genuinely touched to be named MVP.

"It's a great big thrill," said Nitschke, who died in 1998. "It's like a dream. You dream of a thing like that happening to you."

Later that night the menacing linebacker, wearing dark-rimmed glasses and a suit, appeared on *What's My Line*, the prime-time game show that ran every Sunday night on CBS. A group of panelists would ask questions of a guest, trying to figure out his or her occupation.

Dorothy Kilgallen, one of the regulars on the show, asked Nitschke if he was a member of the government.

Arlene Francis, another panelist, said, "He's very quiet and reserved, which would lead one to believe he is with the Giants, but I believe he's with the Green Bay Packers."

Following the game, players talked about the hitting that occurred on Yankee Stadium's frozen field.

"That was the toughest game I ever played in," Hornung said.

Packers left guard Fuzzy Thurston added, "You could really feel it when they hit you out there today, you could feel it in your bones. The Giants were the best today I've ever seen 'em. I thought we were a lot better today too than we have been."

McGee, the team clown said, "That was the hardest-hitting game I ever saw, and I watched most of it. I didn't know a human body could get that cold. And still survive."

The Giants felt the disappointment of coming up short in another championship game, although their performance was significantly better than the one a year earlier.

"We knew it was going to be a hard-hitting game and that's what football was," cornerback Dick Lynch said. "It was a great game just as far as making tackles and just whacking guys. I'm sorry we lost. It was horrible."

"It was a great game," the Giants' Gifford said. "We're still the better team."

That statement was hard for Gifford to defend. The weather had affected both teams, and regardless of the conditions, the Giants had failed to score a touchdown in two championship games against the Packers, who, including the postseason, concluded a two-year stretch with a 26–4 record. In fact, going back to a midseason game in 1961 won by the Packers, 20–17, the Giants offense had not scored in ten quarters against the Green Bay team that truly now was the face of the NFL. The 1962 championship-game victory made Lombardi and his players that much more recognizable throughout the country.

In the end the only words that mattered were spoken by the coach of the winning team.

"I think it was about as fine a football game as I've ever seen," Lombardi said. "I think we saw football as it should be played."

CHAPTER 2

Going for a Repeat

Entering the 1962 season the Green Bay Packers were the toast of the National Football League, a remarkable feat considering that four years earlier they stumbled through the twelve-game schedule winning just one game while having another end in a tie.

The Packers closed out the 1961 season with six wins in their final seven games, including a 37–0 annihilation of the New York Giants in the league championship game, a win that brought the NFL title back to Green Bay for the first time since 1944.

Newspaper and magazine writers from across the country were dispatched to tiny Green Bay to report on the magic that was happening in this little town, whose population of 63,000 wouldn't have filled some of the stadiums in the National Football League. The focus of most of the coverage was coach Vince Lombardi, who arrived after the pitiful 1958 season and turned the franchise around immediately. In just a few years he had turned from obscure assistant into the best coach in the game.

There was little doubt that the 1962 version of the Packers could be special. Seventeen of the twenty-two starters were twenty-nine or younger. While Lombardi preached "team," there was immense individual talent on the roster as ten of the players would eventually wind up in the Hall of Fame.

"We thought we were pretty good; in fact, we were convinced we were pretty good," said flanker Boyd Dowler, who caught a touchdown pass in the shutout win over the Giants in the 1961 championship game. Coming off the championship game the year before, we certainly had our share of confidence.

"We weren't scared of anything, weren't scared of going on the road. In fact, it was pretty fun. Lombardi would tell us we're going to show everybody that they're looking at quite an offense line, that they're looking at the greatest offensive line in football and the best defense in football. He'd say people are going to watch the best pass rushers in the National Football League."

Lombardi knew exactly when to use that kind of motivation to get his team ready for battle. The Packers were coming off a 45–7 win against the Baltimore Colts, their third-straight victory after being upset in the opener in Milwaukee against Detroit.

"We went to Cleveland to play the Browns at Municipal Stadium right when we really knew we were good," Dowler said. "We practiced that Saturday before the game and (Lombardi) huddled us up after our little runaround and said, 'Let me tell you this. Tomorrow there will be 80,000 people who will all be Cleveland Browns fans. Don't let them intimidate you.' Ron Kramer said, 'Coach, I played in front of 100,000 people when I was eighteen years old at Michigan. Let's just go out there and kick their butts.'"

Dowler chuckled at the memory. "Everybody laughed. We went out there, and it was one of the first big whippings we put on a good football team. They had Bobby Mitchell and Jim Brown, but we ran around like we were playing a high school team."

The Packers won that game 49–17 as Jim Taylor rushed for 158 yards and 4 scores. The Green Bay defense limited the great Jim Brown—who would go on to win the rushing title with 1,408 yards—to 72 yards.

That kind of domination was expected to be commonplace in 1962 because the Packers had talent and they had Lombardi, who was not going to let his team get big-headed after winning one world championship.

The Packers reported to camp in mid-July, earlier than most teams. As the reigning champion, they would open the season on national TV against the college all-stars at Soldier's Field in Chicago. The tradition of the NFL champion playing a team of college all-stars from the previous season began in 1934. Following the game, most of the all-stars would leave Chicago and report to teams in either the NFL or the American Football League.

Fullback Earl Gros and guard Ed Blaine, both drafted by the Packers, played with the collegians, whose quarterbacks included future Hall of Famers Roman Gabriel and John Hadl. The game was close through three quarters before the Packers outscored the all-stars 21–20 to put the finishing touches on a 42–20 win. Starr threw 5 touchdown passes, an all-star game record—two each to Dowler and Max McGee and one to Ron Kramer.

"He's a great passer, one of the most underrated in the league," said Otto Graham, who was a pretty fair slinger in his day.

The all-stars came into the game shorthanded at running back. Ronnie Bull, who would play with the Bears, had a high fever and missed the game. Also absent was another player who was watching the game from a hospital room in Cleveland. Ernie Davis, a running back from Syracuse who after the 1961 season became the first black player to win the Heisman Trophy, had been practicing with the all-stars when he started having problems physically. He was hospitalized and later moved to a hospital in Cleveland. He was eventually diagnosed with leukemia.

He had been drafted by the Washington Redskins but was soon traded to the Cleveland Browns, who signed him to a three-year, $200,000 contract. He watched the game with several Browns players, including All-Pro fullback Jim Brown, who also played at Syracuse.

Davis was optimistic he'd make a return to the football field.

"I hope I don't waste too much time," he said in a wire service story that appeared around the country the day after the game between the Packers and collegians. "I'm studying every day. That's all I can do."

In Chicago the Packers surprised Graham by giving him the game ball so he could present it to Davis.

"I always have had a lot of respect for the Packer organization and more so tonight," he told reporters. "That's being professional."

Davis never played a game for the Browns, although he suited up for an exhibition game and was introduced before the game at Cleveland's Municipal Stadium. He died the following spring at the age of twenty-three.

Two days before the Packers left for Chicago, Don Hutson, considered at the time the greatest Packer of all time, spent a day with his old team. Hutson played for the Packers from 1935 to 1945 and was the first great pass receiver in the NFL. He led the team in scoring five times and in receiving for eight of

Coach Vince Lombardi runs the projector as he and his coaches review films in their offices at new City Stadium in May 1962. From left are assistants Bill Austin, Red Cochran, Norb Hecker, Phil Bengtson, and Tom Fears.

the eleven years he played. In 1963 he was a member of the first class in the Pro Football Hall of Fame.

As he watched practice he said he was impressed with Starr's accuracy and said the present Packers team had much more overall talent than the best squads in his day.

"We only had twelve or thirteen real good football players, but this team has thirty-six," he said in a story that appeared in the *Green Bay Press-Gazette*.

Lombardi rode the Packers hard in training camp and offered little praise during preseason wins, calling a performance against Dallas "listless." Never mind that the Pack won all six of their preseason games, extending their streak to nineteen consecutive wins in exhibition contests. He stayed on them because he didn't want his players getting soft.

"He was already thinking about winning three straight championships," Paul Hornung recalled.

Defensive end Willie Davis remembered one of Lombardi's pet phrases as he looked back almost fifty years on that 1962 season. "Once you win a championship you have a target on your back," Davis said. "He'd say it's harder to attain than to maintain."

A Golden Day
Packers 34, Vikings 7
September 16, 1962, City Stadium

Paul Hornung knew how to light up a scoreboard.

In 1960 he ran and kicked his way to 176 points during a twelve-game season, establishing a record that stood until San Diego running back LaDainian Tomlinson scored 31 touchdowns for a 186-point season in 2006.

The following year the schedule was expanded to fourteen games and Hornung again was the league's top scorer despite missing two games because of military obligations. He scored 146 points and was named the NFL's Most Valuable Player. He earned another MVP award in the championship, scoring a playoff-record 19 points on 1 touchdown, 4 extra points, and 3 field goals in the Packers' 37–0 win over the Giants.

That was the game Hornung didn't expect to play. He was serving a tour stateside in the Army and a week before the game called Lombardi, telling him he didn't think he'd get a weekend pass to be able to play. Lombardi called in a favor to the one man who could get his left halfback back to Green Bay in time for the game. The coach had struck up a friendship with John F. Kennedy, who was in his first year as the country's thirty-fifth president. Kennedy was a huge football fan and an admirer of Lombardi. At one point he had given the coach his private number, telling him to call if he ever needed anything.

There are varying accounts of what happened for Hornung to leave Fort Riley to play in the game, but enough proof exists to suggest that the young president did have a hand in making that happen.

In the book *When Pride Still Mattered: A Life of Vince Lombardi*, author David Maraniss writes about a letter from Lombardi to Kenneth O'Donnell, a special assistant to Kennedy. He states that Lombardi expressed his gratitude: "I would like to take this opportunity to thank you for your help in obtaining leave for Paul Hornung so he could participate in the Championship game."

Before Lombardi arrived, it seemed as if Hornung would never live up to the big-game reputation he earned at Notre Dame, enabling him to win the Heisman Trophy in 1956 and to be the overall first pick in the 1957 NFL draft. During his first two seasons with the Packers, he showed flashes of brilliance but earned a reputation as a player who cared more about what he accomplished off the field rather than on it. He gained a total 629 yards in his first twenty-four games.

"I was ready to quit after fifty-eight and do something else," Hornung said. "I hated losing."

Lombardi came in and made Hornung his left halfback, telling the Golden Boy he was going to be used in the same fashion Frank Gifford was used in New York when Lombardi was offensive coordinator for the Giants.

Hornung wound up rushing for 681 yards and scoring 94 points, but some of Lombardi's assistants weren't convinced his heart was dedicated to football. During a five-game losing streak in 1959, Lombardi asked his assistants for honest appraisal of every player on the roster. The notes given to Lombardi were later used in a book compiled by Len Wagner from reports provided by Phil Bengston's son, Jay, titled, *Launching the Glory Years: The 1959 Packers, What They Didn't Tell Us."*

One assistant was highly critical of Hornung: "Not a team player. Has ability to do many things but is very lax. Not a good blocker. Does not make the big play when called upon to do so…I question his value as a top flight football player."

Another assistant added: "Paul is a fair receiver, poor blocker. Could be a great ball player but lacks drive. He has pride. He gets by putting out just enough to do the job. He is a problem as far as training and social life and I don't think he is going to change. If we could get a top pro player and a kicker somewhere, I would be in favor of trading him. I think it would do the team more good."

Lombardi didn't listen. He knew Hornung could be special, and the former Heisman Trophy winner showed signs during the final four games of that season by scoring 6 touchdowns after reaching the end zone just once in the first eight games.

He also threw touchdown passes and was instrumental in helping turn a 3–5 team into one that finished 7–5 and showed signs of becoming special. Hornung was a playboy, and he never did change his lifestyle. He partied hard during the week but was ready on Sunday. He was well liked by his teammates and had a lot to do with the strong camaraderie on the team. As time wore on, he became Lombardi's favorite player. Lombardi famously said Hornung was ordinary between the 20-yard lines but had a nose for the goal line once the Packers crossed the opponent's 20.

There were some games when he was truly spectacular, as he was in the first regular-season game of 1962. The Packers opened up a new season at City Stadium against the second-year Minnesota Vikings with Hornung leading the way. The former Heisman Trophy winner from Notre Dame scored 3 touchdowns on runs of 6, 7, and 37 yards. He also booted 4 extra points and a pair of field goals for a 28-point day.

Hornung rushed 10 times for 67 yards and also completed a 41-yard pass to Boyd Dowler on a halfback option. Packers fullback Jim Taylor rushed for a team-high 75 yards on 17 tries but failed to get into the end zone. He gained 14 yards on the Packers' first offensive play of the season, picking up most of the yardage after a key block by Dowler.

Hornung scored his first 2 touchdowns in the opening period to stake Green Bay to a 14–0 lead. The Packers had a second-quarter drive stall on the 3, and Lombardi elected to let Hornung boot a 10-yard field goal for a 17–0 halftime lead. Remember, those were the days when goalposts in the NFL were on the goal line.

Hornung displayed a strong leg with a 45-yard field goal in the third quarter. Bart Starr, who had an average passing day (7 completions in 14 attempts for 108 yards) hooked up with tight end Ron Kramer on an 18-yard scoring strike later in the quarter. Hornung's 37-yard run early in the fourth quarter gave the Pack a 34–0 lead.

Meanwhile the Green Bay defense did a great job in containing Fran Tarkenton, the Vikings' scrambling quarterback, who had rushed for 308 yards and 5 scores during his rookie season a year earlier.

The Packers line, led by end Willie Davis and tackle Henry Jordan, sacked Scramblin' Fran six times for 52 yards in losses. The secondary also had a big day picking off 5 passes, 2 each by Willie Wood and Herb Adderley and 1 by Hank Gremminger. The Packers also forced the Vikings into 2 fumbles for a total of 7 turnovers.

A day after watching film of the easy win, Lombardi said the Packers offense lacked consistency and that the tackling was "bad."

A few days after the game the *Green Bay Press-Gazette* ran a story about the rival American Football League, which, in its third season, was luring talented players away from the NFL with contracts significantly larger than most of the players in the more established league were playing for.

Dowler, who began his career with the Packers in 1959, admitted that the lure of money would have been tempting had the AFL been in existence when he came out of college.

"I would have very seriously considered the other league," he said. "The idea of a new frontier and the chance to get in at the ground floor plus the chance for more money may have swung me over."

Defense steps up again
Packers 17, Cardinals 0, Milwaukee County Stadium
September 23, 1962

Remarkably, the Packers left the field at halftime leading just 3–0 against a Cardinals team that would finish the season with a 4–9–1 record.

Playing at Milwaukee County Stadium, the Packers' part-time home, the team from Missouri caught the Packers by surprise with a strong defensive effort through the first two quarters, holding the Packers to a 13-yard field goal by Hornung. The Packers drove to the 30 or closer three other times, but Starr had 2 passes intercepted and also lost a fumble.

"Their defense upset us in the beginning," Lombardi told reporters after the game. "We had a helluva time trying to find them. They did a lot of stunting in there. We knew they would be tough defensively. It was new to us. We hadn't seen it before this year."

The new defensive look came from the Cardinals' new coach, someone familiar to those around the Milwaukee area. Wally Lemm was a standout running back at Carroll College, a small school located in Waukesha, twenty-five miles west of Milwaukee. After graduating from college he joined the service and began his coaching career as an assistant at Notre Dame in 1945.

Following one season in South Bend, he returned to Carroll as an assistant for two years and then coached for one season at Waukesha High, which played in the Milwaukee Suburban Conference. He left for the college ranks again and eventually landed in the NFL as an assistant with the Chicago Cardinals in 1956. Lemm later coached the Houston Oilers to the AFL title in 1961 and then returned to the Cardinals, this time as a head coach.

Lemm's defense kept the Packers out of the end zone for a half, but it wasn't strong enough to do it for an entire game.

Lemm actually thought the Cardinals had a chance at upsetting the reigning champs. He didn't think the Packers looked sharp when the teams played during the preseason, and he saw some things while watching film of the Packers-Vikings game that told him Green Bay was vulnerable.

"We all thought the champions were ripe for the taking," he said.

As it turned out, Lemm was wrong, and he was impressed with the Packers.

"They're tough to beat because they have the best balanced team in football," Lemm told reporters. "Great runners in Taylor and Hornung, excellent passing, at least five dangerous receivers, tremendous defense, outstanding kicking. All that plus experience. What else can you have in this game?"

Taylor eventually found openings in the St. Louis line and finished the day with 122 yards in 23 attempts, although he didn't reach the end zone for the second straight game.

Hornung scored on a 3-yard run halfway into the third quarter, and Starr tossed a 17-yard touchdown pass to Max McGee midway through the final quarter for Green Bay's final score.

Henry Jordan (74) collars St. Louis quarterback Sam Etcheverry (14) with help from Bill Forester (71) during the Packers' 17–0 victory over the Cardinals on September 23. Bill Quinlan (83) closes in at left.

The Green Bay defense was stellar, limiting the Cardinals to 16 yards rushing and sacking quarterback Sam Etcheverry five times.

The Packers forced 5 turnovers, 3 fumbles, and 2 interceptions, giving them 12 after just two games.

Lemm singled out defensive tackle Henry Jordan, who was on his way to becoming a consensus All-Pro.

"That Jordan is everywhere and he does everything," Lemm said.

"Willie Davis was hitting 'em before I got to 'em," Jordan said after the game.

That season the Cardinals signed a rookie from the University of Wisconsin named Jim Bakken, who had been a quarterback with the Badgers. Bakken, who had been drafted by the Los Angeles Rams, also was an accomplished kicker and would go on to a seventeen-year career with the Cardinals. He was twice named All-Pro and played in the Pro Bowl four times. He was the first player in NFL history to kick 7 field goals in one game.

After Bakken was cut, the Packers contacted him and wanted to sign him. But since the Packers were the champion team, they had to wait to see if other teams put a claim on him. The Cardinals did and signed the native of Madison.

Recalling that Jerry Kramer booted 3 field goals in the 1962 title game, Bakken said, "That could have been me. I know if I would have been signed by the Packers I would have been their kicker when Hornung got hurt. It's something I don't dwell on, but it certainly crossed my mind."

He very well could have been their kicker for three other championship teams and in the Super Bowl wins over Kansas City and Oakland had the Packers signed him in 1962. Green Bay eventually signed Don Chandler as their full-time kicker and punter in 1965.

"A sleepless night"
Packers 49, Bears 0
City Stadium
September 30

Lombardi had an inordinate amount of respect for Chicago Bears owner and coach George Halas, not only for his contributions to the NFL but also because of what "Papa Bear" did when the Packers were searching for a coach following the 1958 season

It was Halas who strongly recommended to Packers President Dominic Olejniczak that he hire Lombardi, the Giants' forty-five-year-old offensive coordinator.

Halas hated losing, especially to the Packers, but he respected Lombardi for how he turned around the Packers. Green Bay being relevant again helped the National Football League, which was important to Halas, who with others had helped create the league.

During the spring of 1962, he made the two-hundred-mile trip from Chicago to Green Bay to help roast Lombardi, who was being honored by the Green Bay Elks Club.

"We're delighted to be part of this richly deserved tribute to Vince Lombardi," Halas said that night. "Although my role is out of character. In the past when we have come to Green Bay it was not to praise Caesar. It was to bury him. But due to our notable lack of success in arranging the football demise of Vince Lombardi and the Packers, we know that his record will continue for quite some time."

Lombardi was touched, and in his mind nothing could have been finer than to have Halas be part of his special night.

Almost six months later the Bears came to Green Bay for the first of two regular-season games with their most hated rivals with a 2–0 record and a banged-up team.

"Lombardi loved Halas for what he meant to the National Football League, but he also loved beating the Bears," Hornung said. "I loved Halas, too."

Chicago came into the game without linebacker Bill George, who was sidelined with a back injury. Halfback Willie Galimore was also injured and unavailable. Fullback Rick Casares, whom Hornung referred to as "one of the toughest sons of bitches I know," was bothered with a heel injury. Defensive back J.C. Caroline was also hobbling. Had the Bears been at full strength they would have had trouble beating the Packers that day. Without several key players, they were defenseless.

After a scoreless first period the Packers rolled to a 49–0 win. The Green Bay defense was relentless, holding the Bears to 217 yards while recovering 1 fumble and intercepting 5 passes, the last returned 50 yards for a touchdown by Herb Adderley.

The offense was at the top of its game as well, totaling 21 first downs and 409 yards. Taylor needed just 17 attempts to rush for 126 yards. He scored on runs of 1, 2, and 11 yards. Elijah Pitts had his best game as a pro, scoring on a 26-yard run and finishing with 64 yards on 9 carries.

Bart Starr completed 9 of 12 passes, one a 54-yard scoring pass to tight end Ron Kramer. Starr also rushed for a touchdown.

Pitts played the entire second half after both Hornung and his backup, Tom Moore, were injured.

"When I came to the stadium today I figured I'd only be playing on platoons," said Pitts, a second-year player, who was an alumnus of little Philander T. Smith College. "I had trouble hitting the holes in the first half. Then, all of a sudden, I was hitting them pretty well."

In the end it was one of the worst defeats in Bears history.

"They were just too good for us," Halas told reporters following the game. "That's about all you can say. The Packers were just a great team out there today."

A week earlier, when asked by a Los Angeles writer about his rivals to the north, Halas said, "The Packers do not yet walk upon water."

Following the game he wouldn't take the bait when asked how this Green Bay team stacked up against others in the history of the league.

"I never compare teams," he said.

Lombardi was gracious in victory and careful not to say anything that would appear to demean Halas and the Bears.

"We've played good ball games before but everything seemed to work today," he said. "Everything we tried worked."

The only story that wasn't related to the Packers-Bears game on the front of the *Press-Gazette* the next day was a story about the Los Angeles Dodgers and San Francisco Giants, who were preparing to start a best-of-three series to decide the National League pennant. The Giants went on to win the pennant but lose the World Series to the New York Yankees, losing Game seven 1–0. Before he began his professional football career as a player-coach, Halas appeared to be a promising baseball player. He was promoted to the New York Yankees and played right field for twelve games before suffering an injury. A popular myth is that Babe Ruth replaced him in the lineup, but that's not true. Ruth actually replaced Sammy Vick.

Lombardi was working with author W.C. Heinz on *Run to Daylight*, the classic book chronicling the 1962 season. The book came out in 1963, and in it Lombardi wrote that several hours after the game against the Bears, he woke up in the middle of the night, bothered by the whipping his team had inflicted on Halas's club.

All week long there builds up inside of you a competitive animosity toward that other man, that counterpart across the field. All week long he is the symbol, the epitome, of what you must defeat and then, when it is over, when you have looked up to that man for as long as I have looked up to George Halas, you cannot help but be disturbed by a score like this. You know he brought a team in here hurt by key injuries and that this was just one of those days, but you can't apologize. You can't apologize for a score. It is up there on that board, and nothing can change it now. I can just hope, lying here awake in the middle of the night, that after all those years he has had in this league—and he had forty-two of them—these things no longer affect him as they still affect me. I can just hope that I am making more of this than he is, and now I see myself, unable to find him in the crowd and walking up that ramp and into our dressing room, now searching instead for something that will bring my own team back to earth."

CHAPTER 3

Bless His Heart

A Lucky Win

Packers 9, Lions 7
City Stadium
October 7

The Packers appeared headed toward a magnificent season after the first three games in 1962. They had posted two shutouts, allowed just 1 touchdown, forced opponents into 17 turnovers, and had outscored their three foes by a combined 100–7.

Yes, the Packers got out of the starting gate very quickly the season after winning the first championship in the Vince Lombardi era.

"It was easy," right guard Jerry Kramer recalled. "We were just a damn good football team."

Halfback Paul Hornung, who accounted for 28 points in the season-opening win over Minnesota, was leading the league in scoring with 49 points, putting him on pace to score 227, which would smash his record of 176 accomplished during a twelve-game schedule in 1960.

Fullback Jim Taylor, the bruiser who was earning a reputation as someone who enjoyed dishing out punishment, had rushed for 323 yards, averaging 5.6 yards per carry behind an offensive line that was the best in football. Quarterback Bart Starr, firmly in charge of the offense after sharing the job two years earlier, had thrown 3 touchdown passes and run for another.

Fleet-footed Herb Adderley and Willie Wood were in charge of the secondary; tackle Henry Jordan and end Willie Davis, both obtained in trades from Cleveland after Lombardi's arrival, were dominating up front and among the best at their respective positions.

Linebackers Dan Currie, Bill Forester, and Ray Nitschke were also playing well and making it easier for the players in the secondary to concentrate on the opposing receivers and quarterback. Counting the 1961 championship game and six exhibition contests, the Packers were on an eleven-game winning streak and making it look easy.

On the other side of Lake Michigan, fans of the Detroit Lions thought they had a team to be excited about. Entering October the Detroit Lions also had won their first three games, scoring 45 points twice and 29 points in the other game while racking up 119 points, or 19 more than the Packers. That was due in large part to the acquisition of quarterback Milt Plum in a trade with the Cleveland Browns.

The Lions dominated the Western Division through the mid-1950s, playing in four championship games and winning three. Directing the offense was Bobby Layne, the potbellied, hard-living quarterback who on Sundays knew what it took to win. Layne wasn't very swift and his passes weren't pretty, but he had steely determination and a knack for winning.

Layne was leading the Lions to a division title in 1957 when his season ended with a broken leg. Tobin Rote, who later played for the Packers, took over and guided Detroit to an 8–4 record, which tied the San Francisco 49ers for the top spot in the Western Conference.

The teams decided the title in a playoff game won by the Lions 31–27. The following week Detroit simply destroyed Cleveland 59–14 for its third championship since 1953.

Layne was never the same after the injury, and the Lions traded him to the Pittsburgh Steelers in 1958. His departure coincided with two straight losing seasons as the Lions had trouble finding a quarterback who could consistently put points on the board. The Lions finished second to the Packers in 1960 and '61, relying on a strong defense that kept them in most games. The offense was not consistent and failed to average 20 points per game during both seasons.

Milt Plum played college ball at Penn State and was a second-round draft pick by the Browns. He became a full-time starter in 1958 and his personal statistics were respectable for a team that had winning records but couldn't challenge the Giants for the Eastern Division title. Cleveland's Paul Brown, one of the best head coaches in the history of football, eventually traded Plum because he felt the quarterback lacked arm strength.

Plum started out the 1962 season as one of the hottest quarterbacks in the league. In an opening 45–7 win over Pittsburgh, he completed 21 of 30 passes for 250 yards and 3 touchdowns. The following week in a 45–24 victory over San Francisco, Plum was even better, connecting on 16 of 22 attempts for 272 yards and 4 scores.

In week three he threw 4 interceptions in a 29–20 win over Baltimore but did toss a couple of touchdown passes while completing 16 of 30 passes overall for 260 yards. It appeared the Lions had found the quarterback who would give them an offense that could get them back to the championship game.

"He's showing us things we've been begging for," Lions coach George Wilson said in a story in the *Detroit News* the week of the game. "He's got a mighty quick arm and I don't go along with the theory at Cleveland that Milt couldn't throw the long pass. What I like about him is that he has the ability to pick out another man when the primary receiver is covered. He gets the ball to him and he gets it away in a hurry."

The Detroit offense was improved, but it was the defense that put fear into the hearts of opposing quarterbacks, running backs, ends, and offensive linemen. Between the ends were Roger Brown and Alex Karras, both of whom feasted on quarterbacks. The ends were Darris McCord and Sam Williams. Brown was freakishly large for his era, packing three hundred pounds on a six-foot-five frame. It was not unusual to see him tossing a helpless offensive lineman into his quarterback.

In the middle, Joe Schmidt, already regarded as one of the best linebackers in the history of the NFL, was flanked by Wayne Walker and Carl Brettschneider, who had been acquired in a trade with the St. Louis Cardinals before the 1960 season. The Cardinals had been in Chicago but moved after the 1959 season.

The secondary featured safeties Gary Lowe and Yale Lary, the latter eventually landing in the Hall of Fame. They also had excellent cornerbacks in Dick LeBeau and Dick "Night Train" Lane, whom the Lions picked up from the Cardinals shortly after acquiring Brettschneider, who had been with the Cardinals for five years when they were in Chicago. He made the move to St. Louis with his wife and son, but the outside linebacker, who had not stood out while playing on a below-average team, did not stay long in his new city.

"I wanted eight thousand, five hundred dollars," Brettschneider said in the winter of 2011. "The Cardinals wanted to give me eight thousand. Can you believe how things have changed? They said if you don't sign we'll trade you, and of course, they did. When I got to Detroit, George Wilson told me he understood that I had a problem with my contract. He says, 'How much do you want?' I say, 'ten thousand, five hundred' and he said, 'No problem.'"

Before training camp started Brettschneider was approached by Don Shula, the Lions defensive coordinator who would begin his head-coaching career the following year with the Baltimore Colts. Detroit was in need of a veteran cornerback, and Shula picked Brettschneider's brain about whether the Lions should go after Jim Hill or Lane, who as a rookie in 1953 with the Los Angeles Rams had set an NFL record with 14 interceptions.

"Which one should we get?" Shula asked Brettschneider. "I said, 'You're asking a ballplayer? Hell, get Night Train Lane.' And that's how he wound up in Detroit."

Brettschneider fit in with his new teammates and played his best football during his final four seasons before retiring. He eventually became the Lions' personnel director.

"Everybody said you played better over there than you ever did in Chicago," Brettschneider said. "I always said we had ten other guys that were really good. That makes a big difference."

Packer quarterback Bart Starr said he thought the general public always underestimated the talent the Lions possessed in the early 1960s.

"They had an outstanding team to the degree where I don't think enough people realized the depth and the quality of their team," he said during the spring of 2011. "One of my favorite players and someone I later became good friends with was Dick LeBeau. Dick, Joe Schmidt, and a few others like them were examples of the total strength the Lions had. I don't think enough people recognized that. However, we were very aware because we were in the same division and had to face them twice every season."

Schmidt joined the Lions in 1953 and became one of the league's first middle linebackers when teams began making the switch from a five-man front with two linebackers to a four-man line with three backers. Small but extremely quick, he had a nose for the ball and was difficult to block.

"Schmidt didn't have to take a back seat to anybody," Hornung said. "He was quicker than anybody in the middle. They were formidable, no question."

Jerry Kramer added, "The Lions were a good football team, they just never had much of an offense."

In *Black and Blue: A Smash-mouth History of the NFL's Roughest Division*, Kramer told a story that exemplified the leadership Schmidt possessed.

"Joe was a hell of a middle linebacker, a great player," he said. "We were getting set at the line of scrimmage and Alex was down in a three-point (stance) and Joe came up behind him and just wailed him in the ass, just booted him." Kramer handled most opposing tackles he faced but always had a difficult time with Karras.

"I go 'Jesus Christ, Joe, don't piss him off any more than he already is.' It stunned me that Schmidt would do that, that anybody would do that to Alex at that time. I guess Alex understood Joe was trying to get him excited, get him up, get him pumped, and he acted like nothing happened. When you have your captain kicking you in the ass to get you ready for a play, or a game, or anything else, that's indicative of a high level of emotion to me."

Detroit had been the one team that hadn't been terribly hurt by the Power Sweep, Lombardi's pet play, mainly because of how their players in the secondary defended.

"Detroit always played us tough," Dowler said. "They'd give us fits. They'd bring the safety close to the tight end. The other safety, who I was supposed to block, would turn his back on me. If I hit him, it would be a clip. That was one way they could defend against that play."

Brown and Karras were also the toughest pair of tackles that Kramer and left guard Fuzzy Thurston would face. They made running up the middle extremely difficult, not only for the Packers but most other teams in the league.

There was a buzz in Green Bay leading up to the game. Detroit had been somewhat of a pain in Lombardi's side, beating the Packers once in 1960 and again the following year, 17–13, in the season opener in Green Bay. A story in the *Green Bay Press-Gazette* four days before the game informed readers that the Packers defense led the NFL in thirteen categories, including interceptions with 12 and in fewest points allowed. The Lions had allowed three opponents a total of 203 rushing yards. They were allowing a league-low 2.7 yards per carry.

There was no denying that the Lions had talent, something Bud Erickson, the team's publicist made clear when he visited Wisconsin to promote the game.

Those were the days when teams would send their flacks to the opposing city to help supply newspapers with information so stories could be written. What Erickson told the *Press-Gazette* could have been used as bulletin board material by the Packers.

"Well, we think we have the two best defensive tackles in the league in Alex Karras and Roger Brown to start with," Erickson told *Press-Gazette* sports editor Art Daley. "Our defensive unit is all veteran and we made just one change from last year. Sam Williams, who was a handyman in 1961, is playing regularly at right end in place of Bill Glass, who went to the Browns in the trade. The other end is Darris McCord, and he's one of the better ones."

Erickson went on to praise just about every starter on defense. Of the secondary, which appeared to have struggled in the first three games, Erickson said, "Our secondary gave up 305 yards in the 49er game but most of those came on 3 long passes. We had a pretty good lead at the time and maybe they relaxed, too."

Also in the news and all over front pages of papers across the country were details of NASA's fifth manned space flight. Wally Schirra and his Mercury spacecraft circled the globe six times on October 3 in what was the longest flight in the two years that Americans had been flying in space.

A hard rain fell Sunday morning, turning the turf at City Stadium into a mud pit. As was expected, the game turned into a defensive battle. The Lions' Williams was injured, but he was capably replaced by Dave Lloyd.

The Packers scored first, on a 13-yard field goal by Hornung in the opening quarter after a drive stalled on the Lions 6-yard-line.

Detroit recovered a fumble by Starr on the Green Bay 34 in the second quarter and used that to drive for the game's only touchdown, a 6-yard run by halfback Danny Lewis, a former standout at the University of Wisconsin. It was the first time Lombardi's team had trailed that season.

The Packers appeared to be headed toward retaking the lead at the end of the first half. Halfback Tom Moore took a handoff and appeared to be running a sweep when he stopped and lofted a pass toward Dowler, who was wide open in the end zone. Moore's pass lacked velocity and was short. Lary picked it off and the Lions went to their dressing room with a 7–3 lead.

The Packers had two other drives in Lions' territory halted by turnovers although they did pull within 7–6 on a 15-yard field goal by Hornung in the third quarter. The Packers moved the ball, and, despite the rain, Starr had considerable success, completing 18 of 26 passes for 198 yards. But the Packer receivers couldn't get past the talented Lions secondary for long gains. It was the bend-but-not-break philosophy, and the Lions were using it to perfection.

The Packers continued to move the ball, but either turnovers or penalties thwarted potential scoring drives. Brettschneider picked off a pass on a

Darris McCord (78), Carl Brettschneider (57), and Joe Schmidt (56) haul down Packer fullback Jim Taylor (31) during a tough, muddy win over Detroit.

halfback option by Hornung and returned it 11 yards but the Lions weren't able to take advantage.

Meanwhile, the rain affected Plum, who eventually completed 11 passes on 26 attempts for 107 yards. The Green Bay defense also did a good job against the run, holding Lion fullback Nick Pietrosante to 19 yards and Lewis to 30. The only runner who had success was Plum, who escaped the rush several times to pick up first downs. He wound up leading the Lions in rushing with 58 yards on 7 attempts. Overall, the Detroit offense totaled just 199 yards while the Packers gained 319. Plum's fast start to the season was an aberration. Counting the Packers game he threw just 6 touchdown passes in the Lions' final eleven games after leading the league with 9 through the first three.

Lombardi was helpless as he watched from the sidelines. Not only had his team failed to reach the end zone for the first time since 1959, he was knocked down early in the fourth quarter when Pietrosante plowed into him on the sidelines while trying to turn the corner on a running play.

As the game wore on it appeared as if Detroit was going to steal another win against the Packers. Late in the game the Lions moved the ball to their 47 and had a first down as the two-minute warning sounded. Many in the crowd of 38,669 headed toward the exits thinking the Packers offense would not have enough time to score even if it got the ball back.

Among the spectators who left early was Robert Kennedy, the country's Attorney General and the brother of President John Kennedy. Robert was a guest of Wisconsin Governor Gaylord Nelson. As they entered their cars moments later they would hear cheers that signaled the Packers' luck had changed.

Plum handed off twice, once to Lewis and another to Pietrosante. The Lions faced a third and 7 from midfield as the clock approached one minute. During a timeout the Packers players anticipated a pass because twice before on third down Plum had completed passes to keep the drive going. But would he risk a pass again, especially with victory so close?

Packers cornerback Herb Adderley, who earlier in the game had blocked a field-goal attempt by Wayne Walker, dug his cleats into the soggy turf as he waited for the play to begin. Plum took the snap and Lions end Terry Barr came his way, making one fake that didn't fool the fleet-footed Packer defender. Barr continued the pattern and made another cut, slipping as Plum released the ball. Adderley was waiting and made the interception. The Lions had gone a couple of ticks more than fifty-nine minutes without turning the ball over to a team that had forced three opponents into 17 miscues. But one was all the Packers needed.

Adderley returned the ball 40 yards to the Detroit 18. The Packers called 2 running plays before Hornung trotted out to try to take the lead with a field goal from the 26. Center Jim Ringo made a perfect snap to Starr, who handled it easily. He set the ball for the Golden Boy who, as usual, was money with the game on the line. The Packers had a 9–7 lead with just thirty-three seconds remaining.

Hornung admitted to reporters that he peeked earlier than normal after he swung his foot into the ball.

"I couldn't help but to look a little," he said with a playful smile. "You're supposed to keep your head down; I had to look up."

The Lions did have one more chance. Plum got his team to the 45 but time ran out, and a game that looked like a Detroit win instead turned into a gut-wrenching loss and one that would gnaw at many of the players on the field that day for years.

The Packers were 4–0, leading the West by one game over the Lions and the Bears. Even great teams need to get lucky once in a while.

Following the game Adderley told reporters details about the game-changing interception,

"I was playing (Barr) to the inside," he said. "I knew if he cut to the outside I could recover in time. I waited for him to make his second move; no receiver makes a single move. He did and he slipped. I knew he couldn't recover in time to get behind me. I looked upfield at the quarterback and saw the ball coming and I went for it. It was an easy interception. All I had to do was go up and get it."

Lombardi wouldn't comment on the Lions' decision to call a pass. Instead he talked about Detroit's toughness.

"Our fellows had to block the toughest front line foursome in football," he said. "That's quite a job. Nobody runs helter-skelter against that outfit."

He also informed the scribes that Jim Taylor played despite a temperature of 101. The fullback still averaged nearly 5 yards a carry, finishing with 95 yards on 20 attempts.

In the Lions' locker room Wilson said he was responsible for the pass that changed the game.

"I don't want Plum to be blamed for it," the coach said. "We were just going for the first down, and remember we had made two in a row on the same play. Suppose we had kicked the ball? They complete a long pass and kick a 35-yard field goal."

"Milty Plum, bless his heart," Kramer said more than forty-eight years after that game. "He throws a little square out with about a minute to go. Herb Adderley intercepted, Hornung kicked the field goal, and that was that. They were so pissed, they were so disappointed after that game. They were in their locker room throwing garbage cans and shit against the wall. They were going nuts."

More than just garbage cans were being tossed around.

"Alex Karras came in and threw his helmet at Milt Plum all the way across the locker room," Brettschneider recalled. "My feeling was we lost; there wasn't a hell of a lot we could do about it. Yeah, everybody was upset because we felt we should have kicked the ball. The game was there for us to win. It was just a stupid call the Lions made having Milt Plum throwing the ball on third down. We had them beat; we had held them. They just got those 2 field goals. It was raining. The defense played a great game, and it was a disastrous call that did us in. We didn't have a lot of love for the Packers. We should have won that game."

Almost fifty years later the outcome of the game still haunts Joe Schmidt. He and Brettschneider had dinner during the 2010 season, and Schmidt and his former teammate replayed the game one more time.

"Joe says that game set back the Lions fifty years," Brettschneider said.

Many players from that era have trouble remembering games played in certain years. Schmidt is not one of those players. He remembers what happened on a muddy field in Green Bay on October 7, 1962 like it was yesterday.

"That play never should have been called," he said. "That caused a controversy on the team. Everyone blamed Milt Plum. Milt Plum didn't call that play. That play came from upstairs. It was dispatched. Plum threw the ball; Terry Barr slipped. It was a timing pass. Maybe if Terry doesn't slip he catches the ball.

"Adderley was off him; he wasn't close to him. It was not a great interception by any stretch of the imagination as far as I can remember. If Barr doesn't slip or bats the ball down or catches it, it's a different story."

Or if the pass had never been thrown and the Lions ran the ball, failed to pick up the first down and punted, the Packers would have had a tougher time getting the ball into field goal range.

"I don't necessarily think they could have traveled 80 yards on us," Schmidt said. "But again, who the hell knows? That's what makes the game interesting."

Two weeks later the Lions blew a lead against the New York Giants at Yankee Stadium and lost, 17–14. In a span of fourteen days they had played the teams that would eventually make it to the 1962 championship game and lost both by a total of 5 points.

Detroit wound up 11–3 that season, losing their last game to the Bears by a 3–0 score. The Lions defense, as usual, carried the team for much of the season.

Three losses by a total of eight points. But only division champions proceeded to the postseason.

"It was the best team I ever played on," said Brettschneider.

He never won a championship in Detroit but six weeks later Brettschneider and his teammates would have a Thanksgiving to remember in the rematch with the Packers.

CHAPTER 4

How the Team Was Built

When Vince Lombardi became coach of the Green Bay Packers in the winter of 1959, he inherited the worst team in football, one that had compiled a 1–10–1 record during the 1958 season. The Packers not only had a bad record, they were often not competitive, losing seven of those games by 14 or more points. The worst of those defeats was a 56–0 whipping by the Baltimore Colts, who went on to win the league championship.

The franchise, which had won six titles under flamboyant Curly Lambeau, had last compiled a winning season in 1947 when that team finished third in the Western Division with a record of 6–5–1. During the next eleven seasons Green Bay achieved a .500 mark twice and lost eight or more games in the other nine. The Packers hadn't won a National Football League title since 1944. With all the losing they had endured through 1958, that fourteen-year drought must have seemed like forty to Packers fans.

Cleveland Browns coach Paul Brown called Green Bay "The Siberia of the NFL." Red Smith, a native of Green Bay and a columnist for the

49

New York Herald Tribune wrote of the 1958 season, "They overwhelmed one opponent, underwhelmed 10 and whelmed one."

The Packers were terrible but they did possess some players with talent, thanks to Jack Vainisi, who was hired as a scout in 1950 when he was twenty-three. Vainisi grew up in Chicago, where his parents ran a grocery and deli that served as a hangout for some of the Chicago Bears players, who on occasion would be invited to the Vainisi house for dinner.

Young Jack, a Bears fan, had been a grade-school classmate of George Halas Jr., whose father owned and coached the Bears. Vainisi later attended St. George High School where he became an all-Chicagoland lineman and earned a scholarship to Notre Dame, which was coached by Hugh Devore, who earlier in his career had been a line coach at Fordham, which received national attention for a group of linemen called the "Seven Blocks of Granite." Lombardi was a member of that well-known line.

Vainisi played one season before he was drafted by the Army. That and a heart condition detected when he was in the service ended any chance Vainisi would have at a career as a football player.

When Vainisi finished his tour in the Army he returned to Notre Dame and earned a degree. Even though he couldn't play football he desired to remain in the sport. Vainisi got his break with the Packers, whose coach, Gene Ronzani, had been one of the Bears players who knew his parents. It also didn't hurt that Devore was Ronzani's top assistant.

Vainisi was a tireless worker and had a keen eye for talent. When Lombardi arrived, many of the players he coached that first season were with the Packers mainly because of Vainisi, who had scouted them and advised the organization to draft them.

Among the players drafted on Vainisi's recommendation were quarterback Bart Starr; running backs Paul Hornung and Jim Taylor; offensive linemen Jim Ringo and Forrest Gregg; and linebacker Ray Nitschke. He also was involved in the acquisition of safety Willie Wood, who signed as a free agent in 1960. All seven would eventually be inducted into the Pro Football Hall of Fame.

Other players who were starters when the Packers won their first of five titles under Lombardi in 1961 and had been drafted on Vainisi's advice were offensive linemen Jerry Kramer and Bob Skoronski; wide receivers Max McGee and Boyd Dowler; tight end Ron Kramer; defensive tackle Dave Hanner; linebackers Dan Currie and Bill Forester; and safeties Hank Gremminger and Johnny Symank.

The Packers' 1958 draft is regarded as one of the greatest in NFL history, thanks to Vainisi. Currie was selected in the first round, Taylor in the second, Nitschke in the third, and Jerry Kramer in the fourth.

"Sometimes people forget how much Jack meant to the Packers," Kramer recalled.

Ronzani, whose best year was a 6–6 record in 1952, was fired after ten games of the 1954 season. Lisle Blackbourn, a former coach at Marquette University, was eventually hired as his replacement and coached four full seasons before he was fired in 1957 after the Packers went 3–9. Ray (Scooter) McLean was next, and he resigned under heavy pressure after his team was "overwhelmed" ten times in his only season as coach.

Vainisi, who by now was the Packers' personnel director, was asked by team president Dominic Olejniczak to scour the league for head coaching candidates. While the Packers' executive committee came up with a list of college coaches, Vainisi went looking for quality pro assistants. It didn't hurt that he had developed strong contacts with NFL luminaries such as Halas of the Bears and Brown of the Browns, who both told him about Lombardi, a talented assistant with the New York Giants.

Lombardi had joined the Giants in 1954 after serving as an assistant to Red Blaik at Army. There were rumors he might get the head coaching job but that went to Jim Lee Howell, who then hired Lombardi to coach his offense. Lombardi was with the Giants when he unveiled the Power Sweep, which featured Frank Gifford, a former All-American at Southern California. Gifford turned from a good player into a great one under Lombardi, becoming a triple threat, someone who not only could run effectively on the sweep but catch passes and also throw out of the halfback option.

Lombardi's success in New York earned him a chance to coach the Philadelphia Eagles, who were looking for a coach following the 1956 season. He strongly considered the job but on advice from friends and colleagues turned it down because the Philadelphia organization was a mess. He was hopeful that another opportunity would come before he grew too old.

Vainisi convinced Olejniczak to check out Lombardi, so the Packer president made calls, reaching out to Halas and Brown, who both told him Lombardi would be a strong hire. The Packers had a large list of candidates, but it finally came down to Lombardi and University of Iowa coach Forrest Evashevski, who had led Iowa to a win in the 1959 Rose Bowl. The Packers were set to hire the Hawkeyes coach before Evashevski let it be known that he wasn't

From the start of his tenure in Green Bay, Lombardi was in command.

going to coach more than two years. He decided to remain in the college game, leaving the Packers without a new coach.

Olejniczak then turned his full attention to Lombardi, who also was being considered to replace Red Blaik as head coach at Army, which eventually stayed with its practice of hiring only those who had been former cadets as head coaches.

Olejniczak and Lombardi first met in January in Philadelphia, where owners and coaches had convened for the final twenty-six rounds of the then thirty-round NFL draft of college players. Lombardi was eventually brought in to Green Bay, where he met the team's board of directors. He was offered a contract, which he first said didn't include enough money. He eventually agreed on a five-year deal worth $36,000 a year.

Lombardi wouldn't have come had it not been for Vainisi, whom he respected as a personnel man. Because of Vainisi, Lombardi had some potentially strong players. His biggest challenge would be to change the perception that the Packers could not be a successful team.

"We were blessed to have some very talented people but we lacked the leadership and the direction, the discipline and the drive," said Starr, who was drafted in the seventeenth round in 1956. "I think we recognized the direction and the leadership was just not there before coach Lombardi arrived."

After he was hired Lombardi let the Packers board know from the start that this was going to be his team. There would be no meddling from anyone else.

"I want it understood; I'm in complete command here," he said. "I expect full cooperation from you. You will get full cooperation from me in return. I've never been associated with a loser and I don't expect to be now. You have my confidence. I want yours. I'm not against anything that will help the Packers."

Lombardi's first order of business was to assemble a coaching staff. Phil Bengtson, who had been with the San Francisco 49ers, was picked to run the defense. Red Cochran, who had lost his job when the Detroit Lions replaced him with McLean, was named coach of the running backs. Norb Hecker, a former NFL player, would coach the defensive backs, and Bill Austin, twenty-nine, who had been on the Giants offensive line when Lombardi was with the team, was picked to coach the line.

Lombardi then began watching hours upon hours of film of his new players, making notes of who had potential and who probably wouldn't make the team. Hornung had played both running back positions and quarterback, but as the new coach watched on the screen, he saw things that reminded him of Gifford. The player with the blonde curly hair would be his left halfback. The new coach liked Taylor's toughness and thought the former LSU standout could be a punishing fullback.

The Packers used three quarterbacks in 1958: Starr, Babe Parilli, and Joe Francis. Lombardi eventually obtained Lamar McHan in a trade from the Chicago Cardinals. McHan would start the season opener against the Bears, but as the season went on he and Starr split the job while Francis hardly played. Babe Parilli, a veteran who had been one of the starters in 1958, was cut about a week before the regular season.

Months before Lombardi's first training camp the quarterbacks were called to Green Bay to learn about Lombardi's offense. This was going to be all classroom sessions—chalk and a blackboard, no footballs.

Lombardi was decisive and intelligent, explaining his system in a manner that was easy to understand. He taught his quarterbacks how to read defenses, telling them the different adjustments that could be made depending on what they saw on the other side of the line of scrimmage. Starr grasped the system immediately and had a good feeling after the first session with his new coach.

"When he arrived we saw immediately in that first meeting, how he conducted himself. What he had to say was so enlightening and motivating and stirring," Starr recalled. "I've told the story before that when we took a break, I ran downstairs and got on a payphone to call my wife. All I said to her was, 'Honey, we're going to begin to win.' That's what I want to emphasize; it was that obvious."

The rest of the players wouldn't meet Lombardi until a day before training camp began in late July. During his first full team meeting he let it be known that the country club environment in Green Bay was gone. This was not a coach who, like McLean, played cards and drank with the players. His players would act and dress like professionals; tardiness would not be tolerated and neither would negative attitudes. Lombardi's plan was to make his team the Yankees of the National Football League. The players knew from that moment that this new coach was going to be different, very different.

"Scooter was a great guy, but he had no leadership abilities," former Packers end Gary Knafelc said in *When Pride Still Mattered*, David Maraniss's book on Lombardi. "He was not demanding. If you've been around ballplayers, you know they'll take you to the hilt every time. They'll drive you. They'll get everything they can out of you. And we took Scooter in every way."

Lombardi made several trades, bringing in players to fill glaring weaknesses on both sides of the ball. He acquired Fred (Fuzzy) Thurston, a native of Altoona, Wisconsin, who was a backup guard with the Baltimore Colts. He was the Packers' new left guard and would become an instrumental figure in the Power Sweep, Lombardi's pet play. He and right guard Jerry Kramer became known as the "Guardian Angels" for Hornung and Taylor.

Lombardi worked out a five-player deal with the Browns to acquire defensive end Bill Quinlan and tackle Henry Jordan, both of whom immediately improved the defense.

Practices were grueling; most of the players had never been through the type of physical and mental pain they endured under Lombardi. Those who couldn't deal with the punishment were cut. The new coach demanded perfection and was relentless in his pursuit of it. Green Bay dropped its preseason opener, losing 19–16 to the Bears in Milwaukee. They then played five games away from Wisconsin, winning four of them, which gave the team momentum heading into the regular season. When the regular season began, this was his starting lineup for the opener against the Bears:

LEFT END: Max McGee

LEFT TACKLE: Bob Skoronski

LEFT GUARD: Fuzzy Thurston

CENTER: Jim Ringo

RIGHT GUARD: Jerry Kramer

LEFT TACKLE: Forrest Gregg

TIGHT END: Gary Knafelc

QUARTERBACK: Lamar McHan

LEFT HALFBACK: Paul Hornung

FULLBACK: Jim Taylor

FLANKER: Lew Carpenter

DEFENSE

LEFT END: Nate Borden

LEFT TACKLE: Dave Hanner

RIGHT TACKLE: Henry Jordan

RIGHT END: Bill Quinlan

LEFT LINEBACKER: Dan Currie

MIDDLE LINEBACKER: Tom Bettis

RIGHT LINEBACKER: Bill Forester

LEFT HALFBACK: Bobby Freeman

RIGHT HALFBACK: Jesse Whittenton

LEFT SAFETY: Emlen Tunnell

RIGHT SAFETY: Bobby Dillon

The Packers beat the Bears 9–6 at City Stadium, and Lombardi was carried off the field. That was the first of three straight victories, which created a buzz in the NFL's smallest city.

That buzz turned into a grumble among the fans when the team suffered through a five-game losing streak. The quarterback situation was a mess. Lombardi's staff was divided on Starr and McHan, who were splitting time. It wouldn't be until the end of 1960 that Starr was given the job permanently, hitting a stride that would lead him to Canton and the Hall of Fame. The defense, while improved from 1958, was inconsistent. Middle linebacker Ray Nitschke, a future Hall of Famer, was a wild man off the field. There was a point midway through the '59 season when Lombardi asked his four assistants for assessment on every player on the roster. These candid observations were later turned into a book titled *Launching the Glory Years: The 1959 Packers, What They Didn't Tell Us.* Three of the assistants wrote these words for the coach about Nitschke:

"Will always be in trouble and causing trouble," said one coach. "Seems like he will always be too erratic to play defense. I don't know where he would play on offense. Should be good trade material."

Another wrote: "Has physical ability but cannot think. Will never be able to play for us. Trade him."

And one more: "A real scatterbrain, but I believe if it were possible to play him more he could be a good one, particularly as a middle linebacker."

Nitschke almost was kicked off the team the following season. Lombardi had a rule that players couldn't drink at the bar. They could have a drink at a table, but players standing at the bar was forbidden. One day before a road game, Nitschke was standing at the bar when Lombardi and a couple of his assistants walked into the hotel bar. They passed Nitschke, who said hello, but didn't get an answer in return. Nitschke tried sending drinks over, but Lombardi and the coaches got up and left.

Lombardi told his coaches he was going to get rid of the disobedient linebacker. The coaches thought it was a bad idea; Nitschke's play had improved and it was obvious he was needed for the stretch run in the battle for the Western

Division title. Lombardi didn't want to appear to back down from his stance so he told the players about what happened and told them to vote on whether Nitschke should stay with the team or be cut. The players voted unanimously to keep him.

Off the field players kept their distance from Nitschke because he was mean, especially when he had too much to drink. He picked fights with anyone, whether it was a teammate or just an average citizen minding his own business in a bar.

Nitschke eventually changed his demeanor off the field when he met Jackie Forchette, the woman he would marry in 1961. He quit drinking and became a good family man and a better teammate.

Lombardi's staff was also divided on Hornung, whose off-the-field carousing gave the impression he didn't care about football. Some coaches wanted to get rid of him.

There was also strong criticism of some other players.

One assistant wrote of Thurston, "Adequate but not good enough for a top team."

One's assessment of Quinlan was, "Not a mobile player. Does his best when the play comes at him. I don't believe he's a good player for the team."

And then there were these two reports on Starr, who had struggled often when he played during the first eight games. The first: "Not a consistent passer. Not a take-charge type of player. I do not believe we can win with him."

The other said, "A capable fill-in at best. He should be kept until we get a better boy with promise to be worked with, rather than have Starr take up our time."

Lombardi saw something in the fourth-year player and decided to give Starr a long look, starting him in the final four games. Starr had some tough moments but also showed promise. In the season-ending game against San Francisco, the Packers fell behind 14–0. Starr led the comeback, throwing 2 touchdown passes as the Packers scored 36 unanswered points as they won their fourth straight game and finished with a 7–5 record for the team's first winning record since 1947.

Rookie Boyd Dowler eventually became the starting flanker and led the team with 32 receptions, which earned him a berth on the All-Rookie team. Hornung led the team in rushing with 681 yards and the NFL in scoring with 94 points and was selected to the Pro Bowl, along with Forester, Gregg, Ringo, and Tunnell, a perennial All-Pro with the Giants, who followed Lombardi to Green Bay.

There were various All-Pro teams in those days, but those who named first teamers on two of the All-Pro teams were Ringo, Gregg, and Hornung.

"We won those last four games and by the end of the season we were a pretty good football team," Dowler recalled. "One of the big things that happened was picking up Henry Jordan, who really picked up the defense and gave us a pass rusher, he made a real difference on that side of the ball. We went out to the West Coast at the end of the year and played a couple of good games against San Francisco and the Rams to finish 7–5. One of the things Lombardi told us was to come back and be ready to win."

The Packers were ready, and, with few exceptions, Lombardi was going to do it with those who played for him during his first season.

The offense stayed intact. On defense, Hank Gremminger, who replaced Freeman during the 1959 season, was the starting left corner in 1960. The other change in the secondary was at right safety where Johnny Symank replaced Dillon, who retired.

There was one other significant move that would pay dividends during Lombardi's remaining years in Green Bay. In another trade with Cleveland he picked up Willie Davis, who had been an outstanding small-college player for coach Eddie Robinson at Grambling. He gave up A.D. Williams, a player who didn't appear to have a future in Green Bay. It was a steal.

Davis, like Jordan, who a year earlier was also obtained from Cleveland, would end up in the Hall of Fame. Davis gave Lombardi another pass rusher and also a future leader for the defense.

"One of Paul Brown's favorite statements used to be, 'If you don't like it we can always send you to Green Bay, the Siberia of the NFL,'" Davis said with a

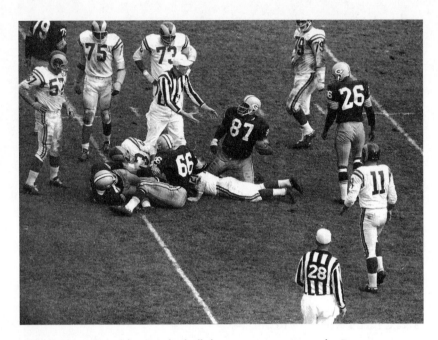

Willie Davis (87) holds onto the ball during a game against the Rams. He was a leader on the great Packer defense of the 1960s, joined by Ray Nitschke (66) and Herb Adderley (26).

chuckle, years later. "I would say that we certainly erased that notion with what would happen in the next several years. By the time I was done playing there, guys couldn't wait to get to Green Bay."

Davis, like Jordan, was popular among his teammates. His role as a leader also made it easier for other black players to fit in when they arrived in Green Bay. Sacks weren't kept when Davis played, but people who have studied film of all the Packers games said he likely had 140 during his ten seasons with the team. More importantly, he won five NFL championships and started in the first two Super Bowls, both won by the Packers.

"I would say that, yes, that trade worked out very well for me," Davis said.

Starr acknowledged that the acquisitions of Jordan and Davis were among the biggest of the Lombardi era.

"Henry Jordan and Willie Davis meant everything to us," he said. "I need not tell you that in order to have a championship team you need to have all the pieces fall into place. People usually talk about offensive players but you have to have a very, very strong dominating defense. Those two men were typical of the quality of players we were blessed with. As a result that was one of the reasons we were able to win so much."

The Packers lost the season opener to the Bears but then reeled off four wins to grab first place in the Western Division. Then there was a stretch in which the Packers lost three of four games, including a 23–10 loss to the Lions in Detroit on Thanksgiving that left them with a 5–4 record with three left to play.

The Sunday after the Lions game, Vainisi collapsed and died in his home, the victim of a massive heart attack. He was just thirty-three years old. The man who had helped build the Packers and was one of Lombardi's few close friends in Green Bay was gone.

"We're all deeply shocked," Lombardi told the *Green Bay Press-Gazette*. "I have lost a close personal friend. I had known him several years before I came here. It will be hard to do without him."

Vainisi was also a friend to the players, someone they could go to during hard times. His death shook the team.

"He was concerned about you. If you had a problem that was the guy you went to," Gregg said in *Mudbaths and Bloodbaths: The Inside Story of the Bears-Packers Rivalry*. "Jack had a way of telling you where you stood. He'd tell you if you were close to not making the team, if you needed to pick it up, or whatever. Jack was really well liked and respected by the players."

The Packers were grief stricken, but four days after Vainisi was laid to rest, they dedicated that day's game to the man who had helped build their team. Starr had one of his best games, completing 17 of 23 passes for 227 yards and 2 touchdowns in a 41–13 romp over the Bears at Wrigley Field.

The Packers went to the West Coast to end the season with games against the 49ers and Rams. They needed a sweep to win the title. The defense pitched a

13–0 shutout in San Francisco. Hornung took care of the offense, kicking 2 field goals and scoring the only touchdown on a 28-yard run.

The following week, in a Saturday game against the Rams, Starr threw scoring passes of 91 yards to Dowler and 57 yards to McGee. Hornung also threw a touchdown pass as the Packers took a 35–21 decision to reach the championship game for the first time since 1944. The Packers trailed 7–0, and then reeled off 28 points.

The headline in the *Milwaukee Journal* read: "Packers Beat Rams, Earn Title Game."

The Packers were happy in the locker room but there wasn't a wild celebration. Lombardi seemed more concerned with 2 touchdowns allowed by the defense after the Packers had taken a 28–7 lead.

"Our defense was physically drained by the emotion involved," he said in the *Journal*'s account of the game. "A lot of these boys had never been on a championship team before. The pressure was new to them. But we'll be ready to play the Eagles."

When the Packers returned to Green Bay on Sunday, they were greeted at the airport by 10,000 fans. They were heroes in a town that hadn't had a team win a division title in sixteen years. The *Press-Gazette* put out a special edition to acknowledge the achievement.

"You could just see us coming together," Dowler said.

The championship game would be played on the Monday after Christmas at Philadelphia's Franklin Field against the Eagles, who just two years before had a 2–9–1 record. The Eagles had a strong mix of youth and veterans. Among the more established players were quarterback Norm Van Brocklin and center/linebacker Chuck Bednarik, the last of the two-way players.

The Packers outplayed the Eagles but lost the championship game, 17–13, in Philadelphia. Taylor scored a touchdown two minutes into the fourth quarter that gave the Packers a 13–10 lead, but Ted Dean returned the ensuing kickoff 58 yards and then scored a touchdown on a 5-yard run that gave the Eagles the lead again. The Packers mounted a last-minute drive that took them to the Eagles 8 before the clock ran out on them.

"We didn't play as well as we should have," Dowler recalled. "I don't know why, whether we weren't mature enough or what. Norm Van Brocklin and Chuck Bednarik and a bunch of those other Eagle players were older."

The Packers lost but it was clear they were now the team to beat in the West. Hornung had a special year, scoring 15 touchdowns to go along with 15 field goals and 41 extra points. He shattered the league's single-season scoring mark with 176 points.

Taylor had his first 1,000-yard season, finishing with 1,101 yards and 11 touchdowns, averaging 4.8 yards per carry. Davis and Jordan applied pressure up front on the defense, forcing opposing quarterbacks to throw 22 interceptions.

Eight Packers made at least two of the All-Pro teams—Ringo, Gregg, Jerry Kramer, Hornung, and Taylor on offense; Jordan, Whittenton, and Forester on defense.

There were a few changes to the starting lineup in 1961. Ron Kramer, who was hobbled during the 1959 and '60 seasons with a bad knee, replaced Knafelc at tight end. Kramer caught 35 passes but his main value was as a blocker, especially on the sweep. Green Bay running backs averaged 4.6 yards per carry in 1960; they improved that to 5.0 in 1961.

"Kramer doesn't get enough credit; he was a helluva blocker and linebackers didn't stand a chance against him," Hornung said.

The biggest shakeup was on defense. Nitschke became more of a fixture at middle linebacker, although Tom Bettis still was in the rotation. Wood, who made the 1960 team as an undrafted free agent, replaced Tunnell at one of the safety positions. And a rookie eventually cracked the starting lineup at left cornerback.

Herb Adderley, an All-Big Ten running back at Michigan State, was the Packers' first round draft choice. Lean and athletic, he wasn't going to replace Hornung in the backfield but the Packers needed to play him.

"I think he backed me up for a while," Dowler, the flanker recalled. "But Lombardi finally moved him to defense."

That happened when Gremminger was injured and Lombardi reluctantly put Adderley at cornerback. He was there to stick. He had an interception in the championship game, and then in 1962, his first full season as a starter, he had 7 picks.

"I was too stubborn to switch him to defense until I had to," Lombardi once said. "Now when I think of what Adderley means to our defense it scares me to think how I almost mishandled him."

The Packers started the '61 season with a 17–13 loss to the Lions at Milwaukee County Stadium, and then roared six straight wins, taking each by 18 points or more. Away from football, tension was growing between the United States and the Soviet Union. President John F. Kennedy activated thousands of military reservists and national guardsmen after the Soviet Union constructed the Berlin Wall. Professional football teams were affected, including the Packers.

Hornung , Dowler, and Nitschke were called away and stationed at camps in the United States. They didn't practice with the team but usually received weekend passes so they could play in the games. All three did miss a couple games each. Hornung, despite missing two games in the new fourteen-game schedule, again led the league in scoring with 146 points. At the end of the season he was voted the league's Most Valuable Player. Dowler caught 36 passes and led the team by averaging 17.6 yards per catch. Nitschke had 2 interceptions and inflicted punishment on any blocker or running back that had any contact with him.

During the middle of the season Jerry Kramer broke his leg, which ended his season. The Packers line didn't miss a beat. Gregg, whom Lombardi would call "the greatest player I ever coached," took over at right guard. Norm Masters, who alternated at left tackle with Skoronski, replaced Gregg.

Taylor rushed for 1,307 yards and scored 15 touchdowns. Starr completed 58.3 percent of his attempts and tossed 16 touchdown passes, leading an offense that scored 391 points.

The defense picked off 29 passes and limited teams to 223 points, holding opponents to 10 or fewer points in six of the eleven wins.

They reached the title game for the second straight year. The opponent would be the New York Giants, Lombardi's old team. The Giants won the East with a 10–3–1 record. Earlier that season the teams met in Milwaukee and the Packers escaped with a 20–17 win.

It was a different story in the championship game. All three of the Packers servicemen made key contributions. Dowler caught a touchdown pass set up by an interception made by Nitschke. Hornung scored a championship game record with 19 points on 1 touchdown, 3 field goals, and 4 extra points. After a scoreless first period the Packers exploded for 24 points, coasting to a 37–0 win to bring the NFL championship back to Green Bay for the first time since 1944.

The headline across the morning *Milwaukee Sentinel* on January 1, 1962 was huge:

"PACKERS WORLD CHAMPIONS!

Bud Lea's lead to the A1 story read: "Why, it was as easy as taking candy from a baby. The Packers ran the Giants off the property Sunday, 37–0, and proved to the football world that they are the very best."

The picture that accompanied the story was of Hornung's touchdown run. The Packers line had made their blocks, giving him a clean shot to the end zone.

The lead story on the sports page was written by none other than Lombardi, in an exclusive deal he had with the paper.

"For a championship game, this was as fine as any team could ever play," Lombardi wrote. "It was a magnificent effort by everybody. Like it had been all year, this was a determined, dedicated team.

"It has been a long season but this is the culmination of plain hard work. We won all the big ones and this was the biggest one of all. The defense was superb all-around to say the least, and the offense speaks for itself on the scoreboard."

Lombardi ended the article with "It was a tough game, more than the score indicates, and it took a big effort to contain the Giants, and to score on them. We have been solidly rewarded for that effort."

Giants coach Allie Sherman did not make excuses after losing to the Packers for the third time in 1961. The Giants had lost a preseason game 20–17 and a regular-season affair by the same score.

"We met a solid ball club, a very good football team, and we don't have any alibis," he said. "They played us better today than in either the exhibition loss or that game in Milwaukee. That was quite a football team out there."

"We were beating people pretty well in 1961," Dowler said many years later. "We were a very good team when we took the field for that championship game on New Year's Eve. We ran the ball effectively. Bart only threw the ball 17 times and completed 10 including 3 for touchdowns. It was like we didn't have to pass but when we did, it was effective. I think Paul, Kramer, and myself were the only ones who caught passes that day."

Dowler had good recall. Kramer caught 4 passes including 2 for touchdowns. Dowler and Hornung each had 3 receptions.

Eleven Packers were honored on the various All-Pro teams that season. Forester, Gregg, Jordan, McGee, Ringo, Starr, Taylor, and Whittenton played in the Pro Bowl. Hornung would have been there, too, had it not been for his Army commitment.

In three seasons Lombardi had turned a team with no direction into one that became the envy of the NFL. The championship game attracted 60 million TV viewers who saw for themselves just how dominating this little team from Green Bay could be.

The Packers were a relatively young team with Ringo (thirty) and Hanner (thirty-one) the only starters not in their twenties.

'"We had a lot of guys who were able to do different things," Dowler said. "We had a lot of good athletes. We didn't have a Bob Hayes, Olympic-type of athlete, any gold medal winners or anything like that, but we had guys with good instincts, guys who were good football players."

Going into 1962, the team was youthful but experienced, talented, and confident. Those aspects helped create a team that would become one of the best in the history of professional football.

"Everybody came together at the same time," said Dowler, who hauled in 49 passes as a receiver and averaged 43.1 yards as the team's main punter. "There were a lot of good football players when I got there. Lombardi inherited a lot of talent, and he added key guys in the right spots. You look at guys like Henry Jordan and Willie Davis, they made 65 percent of our defensive plays. We got Fuzzy. He wasn't playing with the Colts but he could play. It all came together."

"As we went into '62 we were just so strong," Jerry Kramer said. "We were all pretty much the same age. A lot of us pretty much went through the whole thing together, and we all kind of peaked at the same time—Hornung, Taylor, Bart, Forrest, Fuzzy, Jerry, Willie Davis. The whole package matured at the same time and it was a unique point for us."

The Packers were not a one-hit wonder. Lombardi was in the process of building a dynasty. The 1962 team was the one that would be remembered by many as the greatest in Packers history.

CHAPTER 5

"They'll Get Beat"

The sports world in 1962 was considerably different than it is today. Football fans got their news by watching the nightly sportscast and reading the newspaper. They caught glimpses of their football heroes in weekly player and coach shows, but those were mostly filled with fluff stories and game footage that highlighted mostly the good plays.

Today the NFL Network and ESPN are on twenty-four hours a day. Radio talk shows have hosts who try to turn a mundane early season game into the Super Bowl to attract listeners. Newspaper columnists who also must blog to feed Web sites are writing almost daily in some fashion. It's hard to imagine a coach such as Vince Lombardi trying to deal with the constant attention given to today's teams.

The 9–7 win over the Lions was a game that the national media would have dissected throughout the week had it been played today. Milt Plum would have been torn apart for throwing a pass with a minute left, the one Herb Adderley intercepted and returned into Lions territory to set up Paul Hornung's field goal that allowed the Packers to escape defeat. Lions coach George Wilson would have been labeled a bum for having his quarterback make such a throw when a victory over the defending league champion had been firmly in the team's grasp.

Bloggers would have scrutinized Bart Starr for not being able to get the Packers into the end zone. The Packers offensive line would have been attacked for not being able to push back the Lions defenders so the running backs could make it all the way to the end zone.

Yes, it was a different world in 1962. The Packers knew they were fortunate but the lucky escape against the Lions didn't change anything in their minds. They still knew the best team in the National Football League resided in little Green Bay, Wisconsin.

"Detroit was a team that we didn't own like other teams," flanker Boyd Dowler said. "We were fortunate to win that game, but after that we just went on. We still had ten games to play. We knew we were a real good football team."

The Packers also realized that the close win over the Lions was noticed throughout the league and that opposing teams couldn't wait to be the first to derail the mighty Packers, although the team was certainly not thinking that winning every game was possible because Lombardi would not allow that.

"Because of his direction and his leadership I don't think any one of us was thinking in those terms," Starr recalled. "What we were thinking was game by game, week by week, just seeing where that would take us."

The Packers entered the middle part of the schedule knowing that if the Lions could come close, any of the other teams on the schedule were capable of pulling an upset on any given Sunday.

An offensive juggernaut

Packers 48, Vikings 21

Bloomington, Minnesota

October 14

After failing to score a touchdown against the Lions, the Packers tallied 6 against the Vikings during a 506-yard performance, the first time they had topped 500 yards under Lombardi.

Jim Taylor didn't score but he had plenty of tough runs that set up teammates for touchdowns. The Bayou Bull averaged nearly 10 yards per carry, gaining 164 yards on 17 attempts to push his season average to 6.1 yards per carry.

The other Packer runners gained a total of 45 yards on 25 carries, unable to penetrate the Vikings defense. Coach Norm Van Brocklin, in an attempt to slow down Green Bay's vaunted running attack, played eight men close to the line of scrimmage. While Taylor had a good day, he couldn't reach the end zone. In his effort to stop the run, Van Brocklin opened the door for the Green Bay passing game, and Bart Starr took advantage.

He completed his first 10 passes and finished 20 of 28 for a career-high 297 yards. He threw touchdown passes of 15 and 55 yards to Max McGee and one of 18 yards to Dowler that gave Green Bay a 34–7 lead in the third quarter.

Dowler caught 7 passes for 124 yards. McGee, who had been with the team since 1954, caught a career-high 10 passes, which he enjoyed talking about after the game.

"That's a personal record," the former Tulane running back said. "Best I've ever done before was 9. That was in 1954 against Los Angeles when Van Brocklin was playing for the Rams. The Dutchman must be good luck for me. Eight years ago, that's a long time. That's the best ball game I've had since I've been in the league."

"The Vikings played eight men up close there," coach Vince Lombardi said after the game. "There was nothing else you can do but throw. (Starr) was very good."

Starr's performance was remembered nearly fifty years later by right guard Jerry Kramer as one in which he began a path that would lead him to the Pro Football Hall of Fame.

"I always thought one of the reasons we had a helluva year in '62, why we were so strong, was how Bart matured," Kramer said.

"I think the first couple of years he had the luxury of handing off to Taylor and Hornung. Our running game was so strong that he could just hand it off and we could exist on the run. That running game gave him time to mature and develop his confidence. I think in '62 everything came together for him. He reached his peak and stayed there for some time.

"It took him a while to get there, but I always believed that one of the reasons that 1962 team was so capable was because Bart finally came of age."

The game was Starr's best of the season. Because of the way Taylor was slicing up defenses, Starr didn't pass as often as contemporaries such as Y.A. Tittle of the Giants, John Brody of the 49ers, and Johnny Unitas of the Colts. But he was becoming a deft passer and Lombardi's coach on the field. It was about this time that Lombardi would allow Starr to throw on third and 1 when opposing defenses were expecting Taylor to run into the line to pick up the first down.

On those occasions Starr would find Dowler or McGee wide open, and it often resulted in a touchdown.

Packer fans of the 1960s can recall the simple elegance in the voice of Ray Scott, who called Green Bay games on television.

"Starr. Dowler. Touchdown, Packers."

Unlike the first meeting between the teams, the Vikings did not totally wilt when they fell behind. Quarterback Fran Tarkenton, the Vikings quarterback who in his second season was driving opposing teams crazy with his ability to sustain a play by scrambling from one end of the field to the other, had his best game against the Packers. He did throw 3 interceptions but overall he completed 18 of 29 attempts for 288 yards and 2 touchdowns. Unless they were injured, most defensive linemen tried playing every play. The exception was against the Vikings because Tarkenton would at times run up to 60 yards, running all the way to the left and then back to the right in search of a receiver. In pursuit would be some 250- or 260-pound defensive end or tackle who would need a breather after chasing Minnesota's scrambling signal caller.

Tarkenton engineered two scoring drives in the fourth quarter that brought the Vikings within 34–21, the first time all season the Green Bay defense had appeared vulnerable. But just as quickly, the Packers countered with a couple scores of their own.

Starr drove the Packers 66 yards in just seven plays with Tom Moore scoring on a 6-yard run that pushed Green Bay's lead to 41–21. John Roach replaced Starr and led the Packers to their final score, a 7-yard run by Elijah Pitts.

After the game Van Brocklin, knowing he didn't have to face the Packers again that season said this, "They'll get beat and they'll lose more than one," he snarled. "No team is invincible. We took a lot of their running offense away from them. The only (big) run they had was that Taylor thing to the weak side. We took the rest of it away from them."

Never one to shy away from a question, he had this to say when asked to compare Taylor with Jim Brown, the great fullback of the Cleveland Browns: "Taylor's a lot tougher runner. Brown goes down easier. At least that's what they tell me," the Dutchman said. "I've never had to tackle either of them, fortunately."

The Vikings were only in their second season in existence, but they weren't an easy out. They had their first winning season in 1964, going 8–5–1. One of the victories was a 24–23 decision over the Packers.

———————

The Packers did suffer a significant injury that changed at least one aspect of their offense for the remainder of the season. Hornung, who scored the first touchdown of the game, hurt his knee when he was tackled by Vikings linebacker Cliff Livingston. Kramer, the Packers 250-pound right guard, was called upon to kick and responded by making all 6 extra points he tried. He also kicked two field goals, including one from 35 yards.

"I've been fooling around with it in practice because I've never been needed to kick in a game," he said after the victory. "But I'll have to get serious this week."

Kramer took his new role seriously and performed better than anyone would have expected, as he was successful on 38 of 39 extra-point attempts and on 9 of 11 field-goal attempts during the regular season.

More from Moore

Packers 31, 49ers 13
Milwaukee County Stadium
October 21

On most other teams Tom Moore could have been a starting running back in 1962. Drafted by the Packers out of Vanderbilt in 1959, the third-year player backed up both Hornung and Taylor. With Hornung sidelined indefinitely after suffering a severe bruise to his knee while playing Minnesota, Moore was called on to replace the Golden Boy.

His first start of the 1962 season was against the 49ers, who entered the game with a 3–2 record. They had been the last team to beat the Packers, 22–21, in the second-last game of the previous season. They came in with a plan to try to keep the ball away from the Green Bay offense.

For more than a quarter it worked. The 49ers put together sustained drives on their first two possessions, taking as much time as possible between plays, especially during the first drive when they ran 16 plays that required 9 minutes, 56 seconds The Packers defense toughened near the goal line on both drives and the 49ers had to settle for a pair of field goals by Tommy Davis, which provided a 6–0 lead going into the second quarter.

The 49ers were on their way to another score when Willie Wood intercepted a pass along the sideline and, after being tackled, appeared to be kicked by some San Francisco players. A fight nearly broke out and players had to be separated. It served as a wakeup call to the Packers.

They scored 10 points in the final couple of minutes on a 14-yard run by Moore and a 27-yard field goal by Kramer to take a 10–6 lead at halftime.

"That was our plan, to control the ball but the Packers are awful tough," San Francisco coach Red Hickey told reporters. "They forced us to settle for field goals when we should have had touchdowns on our first two drives. They just knock you down and run over you."

The 49ers didn't go away quietly. Abe Woodson gave them a 13–10 lead with a dazzling 85-yard punt return early in the third quarter. That was the only time the West Coast team reached the end zone and the last time they would score in this game.

Taylor took the game over, scoring on runs 25 and 17 yards as the Packers regained control. He finished with 160 yards on 17 carries.

"They didn't do anything we didn't expect," 49ers coach Hickey said. "They just knock you down and run over you. That Taylor's a hard man to stop whether he has blocking or not." Said Taylor, "I knew I was going for some big chunks, but that wasn't the toughest defense we've played. They hit hard but we've been hit harder."

Lombardi admitted to feeling uncomfortable during the early stages of the game.

"San Francisco had us a little scared in the first half, but they were using a different defense, one we weren't prepared for at first," the coach stated. "But we finally solved it with a few minutes left in the first half."

The Packers took a 24–13 lead into the fourth quarter and scored their final touchdown when Starr threw a 9-yard pass to tight end Ron Kramer, who created a spectacle by making a diving catch in the corner of the end zone. Because of the tightness of the field, which was where the Milwaukee Braves played, Kramer sprawled onto the cinders that separated the playing field from the stands.

When asked if he got any cinder burns, Kramer chuckled in front of reporters and replied, "No, but I got a lot of them in my helmet, let me tell you."

Kramer also talked about the Packers' mental toughness after falling behind early.

"I can tell you one thing for sure, that was a hell of a team effort. Everybody hung in there," he said. "This is the tremendous thing about this team. There are so many guys that have a lot of ability, and everybody works together. I think everybody feels the same way."

Moore made a significant contribution with 84 yards in 14 attempts before leaving the game with a bruised shoulder. It turned out to be the best game of his young career.

"It is satisfying because I haven't had too much of a chance to play in my three years here," he told reporters following the game. "I'm just glad I didn't mess up."

Kramer respects the contributions Moore made that season— one in which he was selected to the Pro Bowl for the only time in his career.

"He was a classy runner. I always thought he was a good football player," Kramer said. "He just had the misfortune of being there when Hornung and Taylor were there."

He recalled one play in 1960 when Moore learned about the "necktie tackle."

"We were playing the Bears, and Tommy was a young boy in his first year," Kramer said. "He was a high-stepping, high-flying runner. Well, on one play he went through the line of scrimmage high stepping through. The next time he had the ball he went high stepping again, and either Doug Atkins or Bill George, I can't recall, caught him under the helmet in his Adam's apple. Tommy went up in the air and his head hit the dirt first. After that he changed his running style."

Starr also has fond memories of the way Moore played in relief of Hornung, giving credit to Lombardi for having a strong bench.

"That's a strong indication of the quality of people that coach Lombardi assembled because obviously you need talented starters, but you also need to

Paul Hornung watches from the bench during the Packers' victory over
San Francisco at Milwaukee County Stadium. Injured early in the season,
Hornung suffered a frustrating year.

have people if something happens to a starter," he said. "If someone goes down,
you have to have someone who can step in there and not lose that much, and
Tom was a perfect example. He was an excellent player."

While the Packers improved to 6–0, they picked up a two-game lead on
the Lions, who blew a lead and lost to the Giants in New York, 17–14. The Bears
improved to 4–2 with a win over Baltimore.

Another close call
Packers 17, Colts 6
Baltimore Memorial Stadium
October 28

The Colts were 3–3 and on their way to a 7–7 season when they played the Packers, who had replaced them as the dominant team in the Western Division after Baltimore had won world titles in 1958 and '59.

Many of the players who had helped the Colts to those championships were gone, but they were still formidable. And on this day they gave the Packers everything they could handle.

"We had a great rivalry with Green Bay, I respected them very much," said former Colts halfback Tom Matte, who was in his second season with the team. "They had so many great players, Herb Adderley, Ray Nitschke, Boyd Dowler. They just demanded respect. We took them seriously all the time. There was no taunting, they were just hard-fought football games."

During Lombardi's nine-year run in Green Bay, the Colts beat the Packers seven times—the most wins over Lombardi by any team that played in the Western Division. Sometimes it would be the Baltimore offense, led by Johnny Unitas, that the Packers couldn't handle. Other times the Colts would win close, defensive struggles.

Going into this game Baltimore had been the one Western Division team that that Packers hadn't defeated on the road since Lombardi's arrival in Green Bay. That changed but it was a struggle into a game that turned into a low-scoring battle—one in which both defenses played well.

Baltimore gained more first downs, 18–14; out-rushed the Packers, 151–111 and outgained them in total yardage, 309–252, the lowest output by Green Bay up to that point.

"(Weeb) Ewbank told me after the game that this is the highest he's ever seen a Colts defensive team," Lombardi said after the game. "He said they were that way all week."

The game was a rough one and generated 163 yards in penalties including 89 by the Colts. Lombardi called the Colts defense the best the Packers had faced.

"We didn't move the ball as well today against the Colts as we did against Detroit, even though we didn't score a touchdown against the Lions," Lombardi said. "They didn't show us anything we hadn't expected, but they really went all out. Everybody's up for us, and it's getting tougher every Sunday."

While the Colts offense had some success, it couldn't get into the end zone, scoring on a pair of field goals by Dick Bielski. They drove into Packer territory seven times but 2 drives came to a halt by fumbles caused when quarterback John Unitas couldn't execute a handoff with halfback Lenny Moore.

The teams were tied at 3–3 after the Colts scored on a field goal 51 seconds before halftime. Aided by two Baltimore penalties, the Packers reached the end zone in just 3 plays, scoring on a 25-yard pass from Starr to Ron Kramer, who was having a special season.

After the Colts pulled within 10–6, in the third quarter the outcome remained in doubt until Taylor ripped off a 37-yard scoring jaunt with six minutes remaining.

The game was played in front of a crowd of 58,000 full-throated spectators, who booed the Packers from the moment they walked onto the field. Some of the Packers reacted differently.

Taylor bowed to the fans as they booed him when he left the field after the game; Starr was upset because he had to signal for the fans to be quiet early in the game when the booing made it too hard for him to call his plays.

"They're poor sports," he told reporters after the game. "That's just terrible. The flankers can't hear the signals and I can't change up at all."

Ron Kramer was knocked dizzy when he ran into—of all people—Packers teammate and right tackle Forrest Gregg.

"He was going one way and I was going the other way and we just met when our paths crossed," Gregg said. "I've never been knocked that hard by anybody."

Following the game many Colts said the Packers wouldn't go unbeaten, and a few of them predicted Green Bay would be beat by the Lions on Thanksgiving.

A tougher time in Chicago

Packers 38, Bears 7
Wrigley Field
November 4

The Packers went to the big city unbeaten and left the same way, although they needed a huge second half after the Bears played them practically even for most of the first thirty minutes.

The score was knotted at 7–7 when Ray Nitschke picked off a pass by Rudy Bukich and ran 26 yards to the Chicago 18. That set up a 17-yard field goal by Jerry Kramer that gave Green Bay 10–7 lead at intermission.

Taylor provided the only scoring in the third quarter with a 1-yard plunge for a 17–7 lead going into the final fifteen minutes.

The fourth quarter was dominated by the Packers, who scored 3 touchdowns, including 2 by Taylor, his third and fourth on a cold, windy afternoon on Chicago's north side.

The Bears played considerably better than they did at Green Bay, where they were humiliated by a 49–0 score. The Chicagoans were their own worst enemy in this game, turning the ball over seven times, four by fumbles and three on interceptions by Green Bay defenders.

One of those turnovers helped turn the game around. The Packers were clinging to a 10–7 lead when a punt by Dowler bounced off the back of Bears return specialist Roosevelt Taylor and was recovered by Packers center Jim Ringo, which set up the 1-yard run by Taylor.

The wind affected the punt, and Taylor ran up thinking it was going to bounce short. He never got a hand on the ball but it bounced off his back.

"That was one of the most freaking plays in the books," Bears coach George Halas said after the game. "A player gets hit in the back with the ball. He was facing north and the ball was coming from the south."

Halas wasn't particularly complimentary of the Packers when asked if they were a super team.

"They weren't one until that particular play in the third quarter," he said dryly. "We were in it until then. In fact, we were in great position, it was a short punt."

The Packers' ground game accounted for 215 yards, almost twice as many as the week before in the 11-point win at Baltimore. Taylor rushed 25 times for 124 yards, giving him 934 for the season.

The win gave the Packers a series sweep of their biggest rival for the second straight year. Counting the 49–0 win in the first game, the Packers outscored Chicago 87–7 in the two games between the teams in the 1962 season.

Lombardi, though, conceded this game was tougher than the final score indicated.

"The Bears were tougher, especially on defense, than they were in the first game in Green Bay," he said. "You know, they trailed only 10–7 well into the third quarter, so we had to stay in there."

The large contingent of Chicago sportswriters peppered Lombardi with questions about the possibility of his team winning all fourteen regular-season games.

"I don't know, we're just going to play 'em one at a time, that's all we can do," he responded to the first question.

That wasn't good enough for members of Chicago's Fourth Estate, who kept asking until they got an answer.

"I think it's highly improbable, let's put it that way," Lombardi said. "Each opponent seems to be aroused and makes a maximum effort to stop us."

A Thorough Whipping
Green Bay 49, Philadelphia 0
Franklin Field
November 11

In what may have been the most dominating win under Vince Lombardi, the Packers set a league record with 37 first downs. They also gained a franchise-record 628 yards while limiting the Eagles to 3 first downs and 54 total yards.

Jim Taylor ran for 141 yards and scored 4 touchdowns for Green Bay, which posted its third shutout of the season and improved to 9–0.

(A complete account of this game can be found in the next chapter).

A perfect 10
Packers 17, Colts 13
Green Bay City Stadium
November 18

The night before the Packers' tenth game, Curly Lambeau, who founded the Packers and coached them to six NFL titles, was honored at the Green Bay Elks Club by being inducted into the Wisconsin Hall of Fame.

Many of the players who had played for him were on hand as was NFL Commissioner Pete Rozelle. Lombardi was also there and handed Lambeau the letter of certification into the hall.

"Curly Lambeau has a record that will hardly ever be equaled," Lombardi told the crowd of seven hundred. "The Packers have a proud, a great tradition, one started by Curly Lambeau. For this tradition, this proud tradition, we are thankful. This is one of the things that helps us win."

It was somewhat ironic that Lombardi was there to toast Lambeau. Privately he disliked the former Green Bay coach because of Lambeau's reputation as a womanizer. He also didn't like it when the headlines weren't about his team. Former *Press-Gazette* sports editor Art Daley, who passed away in 2011, liked to tell the story of when Lambeau died in 1965. For several days the paper wrote glowingly of his contributions to the Packers. That coverage bothered Lombardi, as did Daley's decision to change the cover of the Packers Yearbook that year to a photo showing Lombardi shaking hands with Lambeau.

Lombardi refused to talk to Daley for nearly a year before he finally ended the feud. "I can't stay mad at you; you're too nice a fellow," he told Daley.

The day after the banquet Lambeau and nearly one hundred men who previously played for the Packers celebrated Homecoming at City Stadium. It was also "Hawg Hanner Day" as the Packers honored their long-time defensive end although he would play for two more years.

What the former Packers witnessed was a gritty effort by the Packers, who were forced to use backup center Ken Iman at left linebacker when Nelson Toburen suffered a neck injury. Toburen was playing for Dan Currie, who had been injured the previous week in Philadelphia.

For the second time that season the Colts outgained the Packers and held Taylor to a season-low 44 yards in 19 carries. The Colts rolled up 380 yards, the most allowed by the usually stingy Green Bay defense. But it was the same defense that stopped the Colts three times inside the 10-yard line.

In the first quarter Nitschke recovered a fumble by R.C. Owens on the Green Bay 2. In the second quarter with the Packers leading 10–3 the Colts had a first and goal on the Packers 1. Three running plays, no yards. On fourth down Bill Forester threw quarterback Johnny Unitas for a 13-yard loss, the first of 4

Linebacker Bill Forester sacks Baltimore quarterback Johnny Unitas during the second quarter of Green Bay's victory over the Colts on November 18.

sacks he had that day. Sacks weren't kept as an official record in that era, but the *Press-Gazette* speculated it may have been a team record.

"Things kind of came our way," Forester said after the game. "We were in a red-dog type of defense where we were shooting the linebackers quite a bit. I got Unitas scott free a couple of times, and a couple of times I went through the fullback."

Forester's big afternoon did not go unnoticed by his coach.

"That, by the way, is as fine a football game as I've ever seen Bubba Forester play," Lombardi said. "Bubba played a fine game; he made some real big plays today."

Trailing 17–13 with four minutes remaining in the game, the Colts drove to the Packers 7-yard line. On fourth down Unitas threw to Jimmy Orr in the end zone, but the play was broken up by cornerback Herb Adderley.

"They played us tough in both games that year," recalled Dowler. Outside of Detroit they were our toughest competition. We always seem to have tough games with Baltimore."

The highlight of the game was a 103-yard kickoff return by Adderley after the Colts' Bielski kicked a field goal to give his team a 3–0 lead in the first quarter. After catching the ball 3 yards deep in the end zone, Adderley took off. He received a couple of key blocks, including one from Iman. Once in the open he was off for the second-longest return in Green Bay history. The record was 106 yards in 1956 by Al Carmichael.

"On my last cut I just saw a green jersey (Iman)," Adderley told reporters. "I just cut off that green jersey and saw daylight. I've never had a run like that before. Without a doubt it was my longest."

The Colts had a 13–10 lead, but less than a minute into the fourth quarter, Moore scored on a 23-yard run on a play that fooled the Colts. Starr made a terrific fake handoff to Taylor, who was swarmed by several Baltimore defenders. Starr then gave the ball to Moore, who had clear sailing to the end zone.

Lombardi called it the Packers' toughest game. He credited the Baltimore defense for taming his offense twice in the same season. "It was just aggressive defense," he said. "They did nothing different than they did in Baltimore."

Baltimore coach Weeb Ewbank displayed a sense of humor when he talked about some of the bad breaks his team had during the game.

"I only went to church once today, I should have gone three times judging from the way the ball was bouncing out there today," he said. "One time the ball bounced an extra 20 yards on a Dowler punt when it looked like it was going out of bounds, and another time one of his punts rolled dead on our 2-yard line instead of going in the end zone."

He then turned serious.

"The Packers have a good football team," Ewbank said. "It was no disgrace to lose to them."

As usual Lombardi sidestepped questions about an unbeaten season. His team had four games remaining, with the first coming up in four days in the annual Thanksgiving Day clash in Detroit against the Lions.

CHAPTER 6

Payback

Through the first eight games of the 1962 season, the Packers were clearly the class of the NFL. Undefeated, they already had posted 2 shutouts and had held the Baltimore Colts and San Francisco Giants without a touchdown from the line of scrimmage. Five opponents failed to gain 200 or more yards of total offense. The Green Bay offense had been unstoppable in most games, averaging 31 points, equaling or eclipsing that total five times.

Yes, they were already well on their way to a superb season going into a game on November 11 against the Philadelphia Eagles whose 1–6–1 record was the worst in the Eastern Conference. This could have been a game where a great team overlooked an inferior foe; especially with a couple of games against Western Conference rivals Baltimore and Detroit on the horizon.

That, though, rarely happened under Vince Lombardi, who treated all opponents with equal respect. A letdown also wasn't going to happen on this day for another reason.

"We were still pissed at the Eagles from that game in 1960," right guard Jerry Kramer recalled. "We were going to play that game all over again."

Kramer was referring to the 1960 NFL championship game, played on December 26 at Franklin Field in Philadelphia. The Packers had won the Western Conference with an 8–4 record in Lombardi's second season as coach. Green Bay was two years removed from a 1–10–1 season, which was why the NFL's most-northern outpost was referred to as the "Siberia of the NFL."

Scooter McLean quit before he was fired and replaced by Lombardi, the tough Italian from Brooklyn who made a name for himself as offensive coordinator for the New York Giants. Lombardi had an immediate impact, guiding the Packers to a 7–5 record while changing the cushy lifestyle enjoyed by the players under McLean.

The 1960 team, led by Paul Hornung and Jim Taylor, won its final three games to earn Green Bay a place in the championship game for the first time since 1944. The Eagles were led by quarterback Norm Van Brocklin, who would retire following that game and become coach of the expansion Minnesota Vikings, and by linebacker Chuck Bednarik, the veteran, who like Van Brocklin, was destined for the Pro Football Hall of Fame.

The Eagles lost their first game of the season and then reeled off nine straight wins on their way to a 10–2 record to dethrone the New York Giants as champions of the Eastern Division.

The title came as somewhat of a surprise; the Eagles had a losing record two years earlier and were a respectable 7–5 in 1959. Going into 1960, though, they weren't considered more than a dark-horse contender to reach the title game. The teams to beat were Cleveland and New York. The Eagles earned a reputation as a comeback team that season, rallying for wins in six games during the nine-game winning streak.

Despite having a better record than the Packers and home-field advantage, Philadelphia was picked as a 2-point underdog by Las Vegas odds makers. From the start it looked like the boys in Vegas knew what they were talking about. Packers defensive end Bill Quinlan intercepted a lateral pass by Van Brocklin at the Eagles 14 on the opening play of the game.

The Packers ran four straight running plays, failing to pick up a first down, the first of two occasions when Lombardi would not go for a field goal inside the Eagles 10. The Eagles' only touchdown in the first half came on a 37-yard pass from Van Brocklin to flanker Tommy McDonald, who was only able to make the play because Packers safety Hank Gremminger slipped, allowing McDonald to run by him.

The Packers trailed at halftime 10–6, missing an opportunity at the end of the half when Hornung was wide on a 13-yard field goal attempt after the Packers had driven to the Philadelphia 6-yard line. Green Bay took the second-half kick and the offense looked relentless, driving inside the Eagles 10 before facing fourth down. Again, Lombardi opted to try to pick up the first down rather than let Hornung attempt a field goal. Again, the Eagles held, much to the delight of the crowd of 67,325, at the time the second-largest in NFL playoff history.

Starr, who was showing great poise in his first championship game, threw a 7-yard touchdown pass to McGee early in the fourth quarter as the Packers took a 13–10 lead. Any excitement that Packers felt was short-lived as Ted Dean took the ensuing kickoff 58 yards to give the Eagles good field position. Van Brocklin didn't waste the opportunity, guiding his team toward the end zone before Dean capped the drive with a 5-yard run to give the Eagles a 17–13 lead with 5:21 remaining.

Green Bay got the ball back and began driving, but the drive came to an abrupt halt when Bednarik forced McGee into a fumble at midfield.

The Packers got the ball back one more time with 70 seconds remaining after forcing the Eagles to punt. Starting from his own 35, Starr passed for 2 first downs, eventually driving to the Eagles 17 with 17 seconds remaining.

With no time outs left, Starr went back to pass. With his ends covered, he dumped a short pass to Taylor, who broke two tackles before getting to the 10. Bednarik was waiting for him, and the two collided with Taylor hitting the turf at the 8.

Taylor fought to get up but Bednarik stayed on top of him as the final seconds counted down.

Three, two, one....

"Taylor, you can get up now," the linebacker said when the gun sounded. "The damn game is over."

Philadelphia 17, Green Bay 13.

Moments later as Hornung consoled Taylor, Bednarik stepped between them and wrapped both in a hug, telling them they'd win the championship in 1961.

The Packers had outplayed the Eagles, picking up 22 first downs to 13 for Philadelphia and more totals yards, 401 to 206. Taylor rushed for 105 yards, leading a ground attack that averaged more than 5 yards per carry while rushing for 223 yards. Despite those numbers the Packers were able to score just 13 points.

Lombardi, who would confide to friends that he cost his team 6 points by going for first downs rather than kicking field goals, addressed his team in a quiet locker room after they left the field. "Gentleman, this will never happen again. You will never lose another championship game."

He also could have said they'd never lose again to the Eagles. Lombardi had a long memory, and even almost two years later, going against a Philadelphia team that was without many of the players who helped win the 1960 championship, the coach was still haunted by coming up 8 yards short of a championship.

Those who suited up for the Eagles on that November day in 1962 paid the price for the win the last time the teams met. In what may have been the most dominating performance by the Packers during their nine years with Lombardi, they absolutely destroyed Philadelphia 49–0.

The Packers did all of their scoring in the first three quarters. The 49-point margin did not reflect how truly one-sided this game was. It was an old fashion whipping, plain and simple.

The Packers set a league record with 37 first downs while holding the Eagles to 3. They also gained a franchise-best 628 yards of total offense while limiting Philadelphia to 54 yards. They played as if they truly wanted to punish the Eagles for what had happened on December 26, 1960. Green Bay's 7 touchdown drives covered 86, 89, 85, 76, 71, 66, and 65 yards, respectively.

Almost forty-eight years after that performance, Boyd Dowler, a flanker for the Packers that day, was surprised when he heard those totals.

"Is that right, 600 some yards?" he asked in amazement. "I know we just ran through them. We were awful mad at them for beating us in that championship game. It wasn't the same Eagle team, but there were some players who played in that championship game."

The Packers didn't need any reminders from their coach as they prepared for the ninth game of the season. There was a quiet determination. Every man who was on the field against the Eagles on the day after Christmas two years earlier still remembered the feeling of emptiness as they left Franklin Field without a championship.

Lombardi didn't need to drag out film of that game or remind his players of the 4-point loss.

"No, he didn't need to say anything. We were so disappointed after that game," Kramer said. "We really felt we should have won that game. There really wasn't any need for much conversation. We were strong and confident and pretty much had everything going for us. He was leading the band. We were highly pissed about that Eagles game still."

The Packers took the opening kickoff and efficiently moved down the field, picking up 3 first downs before Starr had a pass intercepted by Irv Cross. But that was one of the few mistakes made by Lombardi's men.

After stopping the Eagles on the first of several 3 and outs, the Packers then drove 86 yards for their first score, which came on a 2-yard run by Tom Moore with 4 minutes 25 seconds remaining in the first quarter.

Moore, a third-year halfback out of Vanderbilt, started in place of Hornung, who had been sidelined four games earlier with a knee injury. Hornung played against the Eagles but Moore was on the field for most of the first three quarters and had one of his best games in a Green Bay uniform.

He also scored on a 7-yard run and threw a 25-yard scoring pass to Dowler on a halfback option that made the score 28–0 in the second quarter.

"Tom was a fine football player, and he really did a nice job filling in for Paul, who was hurt most of the season," Dowler recalled.

Near the end of the half Taylor scored his second touchdown that gave the Packers a 35–0 lead.

As the teams walked to their respective locker rooms at halftime, Bednarik sidled up to Packers assistant coach Tom Fears and asked him when the Packers were going to put in their "scrubs."

"Tom just kept a straight face and said, 'Chuck, we don't have any scrubs,'" Bednarik told reporters after the game.

The Eagles didn't pick up a first down until late in the opening half. The Packers continued the beating in the third quarter with two more sustained drives that ended in touchdowns. Taylor scored both, on runs of 5 and 4 yards.

Taylor would go on to lead the league in scoring and in rushing and earn the league's Most Valuable Player Award. Against the Eagles he wound up with 141 yards in 25 attempts and 4 scores. Moore rushed fourteen times for 49 yards as the Pack totaled 294 yards on the ground. Starr completed 15 of 20 passes for 274 yards.

In addition to pitching a shutout the Packers sacked Philly quarterbacks four times. One of those who played was Sonny Jurgensen, who seven years later would play for Lombardi when the coach came out of a one-year retirement to coach the Washington Redskins one year before dying of colon cancer on September 3, 1970.

After the game Lombardi said his team put forth "a workmanlike performance."

When asked how his team compared to some of the other great teams he'd seen, the coach snapped, "Comparisons are odious. That's all I'd like to say about that."

Emlen Tunnell, an All-Pro safety with the Giants who followed Lombardi to Green Bay and played three seasons and retired after the 1961 season, was in the press box scouting for the Giants.

"They're the greatest I've seen," he said.

The Packers had a chance to break the 50-point barrier in the fourth quarter. Wide receiver Max McGee, who also served as the Packers' punter, took off on a 36-yard run out of punt formation to the Eagles 14 because the Eagles didn't apply any pressure.

Two years earlier in the championship game with the Packers trailing 10-6, McGee gained 35 yards out of punt formation when the Eagles didn't attempt to punt. He ran into Eagles territory and set up a touchdown that gave the Packers a 13–10 lead.

"No, I didn't have any intention of doing that," he said of his run in the 49-point win. "We had enough scores….But they weren't covering as I started to punt. I made another motion to punt and they still didn't come up so I took off."

Kramer, who was doing a fine job as Hornung's replacement on extra points and field goals, was perfect on all 7 of the extra-point attempts. Lombardi let Hornung try a field goal attempt a few plays after McGee's run, but the kick from the 25 was low.

Bednarik, who was in the fourteenth and final season of a brilliant career, said of the Packers, "This is one of the greatest teams in the history of the league. They're superb. That's the word for it." Bednarik had not yet said he was going to retire. He was asked that if a loss such as this would move him in that direction.

"A game like this makes me think," he said. "I just say, 'Chuck, old boy, only five more games left this season.' But, that's as far as it goes. I'm not thinking of retiring just because of today. It's discouraging but there'll be other days."

McDonald, the Eagles All-Pro flanker who entered the game third in the league in receptions with 41, caught just 1, as he was smothered most of the day by cornerback Herb Adderley.

"They're so great, I don't think I could make their rinky-dink team," McDonald said. "If I was on that squad I'd probably be chasing punts and kickoffs."

Some of the Eagles said that it would take an NFL all-star team to beat the Packers.

"But no one would be crazy enough to play on that team," McDonald said.

CHAPTER 7

The Power Sweep

T he Green Bay Packers could do just about anything they pleased on both sides of the ball during the 1962 season.

The defense was superb. Defensive tackle Henry Jordan and Willie Davis created havoc up front; middle linebacker Ray Nitschke destroyed any opponent in his path. The secondary, led by cornerback Herb Adderley and safety Willie Wood intercepted 31 passes and forced 50 turnovers, both league highs.

The offense had the best line in football; quarterback Bart Starr led the league in passing percentage, and fullback Jim Taylor rushed for 1,474 yards and was named the NFL's Most Valuable Player.

Yet when people remember the Packers of the 1960s, they're more likely to remember the play that made guards Jerry Kramer and Fuzzy Thurston household names in Wisconsin: The Lombardi Power Sweep.

Offensive linemen usually live in obscurity; on the Packers they were stars, especially Kramer, No. 64, the big guy on the right side, and Thurston, who wore No. 63 and was shorter and more compact but just as dangerous once he pulled to the outside and looked for a helpless cornerback or safety.

Jerry Kramer (64) and Fuzzy Thurston (63) lead fullback Jim Taylor (31) on the sweep, which became the team's trademark play.

Every player was involved: the tackles, ends, and center all had assignments, and if one was missed the play would fail. When executed to perfection, Kramer and Thurston would be downfield, ahead of either Taylor or Hornung, often leading the ball carrier into the end zone.

"It was a fascinating play that had so many variations; you could go almost anywhere," said Kramer, the athletic right guard who was voted to the NFL's fifty-year anniversary team in 1969.

"I see pictures today. Fuzzy and Hornung and I were in such sync. You'll see pictures of the sweep, and all three of us will be planting a foot at the same time, at the same instant. We just saw things and turned at the same time."

The Packers scored an NFL-high 415 points during 1962, mainly because of the effectiveness of the Lombardi Sweep. The Packers led the league in rushing with 2,460 yards, averaging 4.7 yards per try.

The Packers scored 50 offensive touchdowns with 36 coming on running plays. The St. Louis Cardinals were a distant second with 20 touchdowns. Many teams were throwing more. In Green Bay the name of the game was power football with the sweep being the team's signature play.

Kramer and Thurston were the guards. Jim Ringo, a perennial All-Pro and future Hall of Famer, called the shots at center. Forrest Gregg, another future Hall of Famer, was at right tackle. Bob Skoronski and Norm Masters shared left tackle. Another key blocker was tight end Ron Kramer, whose weight fluctuated between 250 and 265 pounds.

"Kramer just owned the linebackers," flanker Boyd Dowler recalled.

When Lombardi left the New York Giants as their offensive assistant for the head coaching position with the Packers he brought the play with him. In New York he built the sweep primarily for left halfback Frank Gifford, a gifted runner who also had the ability to make a precise throw, adding another dimension to the play.

Lombardi joined the Giants in 1954, a year after they finished last in the National Football League in rushing. In addition to Gifford, Lombardi also wanted to utilize the talent of young backs Mel Triplett and Alex Webster. He introduced his offense to the sweep, and it became the Giants' key play in 1956, which culminated with the team claiming the NFL title with a 47–7 win over the Bears.

Lombardi didn't invent the play; it only seemed as though he had. The Los Angeles Rams had been running a sweep with the guards serving as the lead blockers. When Lombardi was in college he saw variations of it in the old single-wing offense.

Lombardi's techniques, though, were different than most offensive coaches. He gave his linemen wider splits, forty inches apart. Not thirty-six, thirty-eight, or thirty-nine, but forty. He could look at the linemen and tell if they were even two inches off one way or the other.

Lombardi's version of the sweep also gave more freedom to his linemen depending on how the opposition was playing. If the opposing outside linebacker was pushed to the left, the ball carrier ran to the right.

"Lombardi was a live wire. I can't remember a single meeting when he didn't break the chalk on the board putting up a play," former Giants end Pat Summerall wrote in *Giants: What I Learned From Vince Lombardi and Tom Landry*. "But it wasn't all about show; the man knew what he was talking about like no offensive coordinator I had ever known. His plays were precise down to the length of the first step the offensive end should take to achieve his block and how he should time it so it was executed just as the quarterback began his first step away from center and out of the path of the pulling guards."

When Lombardi came to Green Bay he watched countless hours of film of the players left over from the 1–10–1 team in 1958. What he saw sometimes discouraged him—ends dropping easy passes, linemen failing to finish blocks. He also saw encouraging signs. Ringo, although small, was quick at center and intelligent. Young Jerry Kramer, who was entering his second season, had the potential to be a very, very good right guard. Thurston, acquired in a trade with Baltimore where he played little, had played basketball in college and so had some athleticism.

Lombardi needed a halfback in the mold of Gifford. Hornung had done little as a pro after winning the Heisman at Notre Dame. During his first two years with the Packers he had been used at quarterback and both running back positions. While breaking down film with his coaches, Lombardi saw something in Hornung. He had instincts as a ball carrier, and he could throw, which would give defenses something to think about as Hornung made his way to the outside. Hornung also ran with power.

The Power Sweep was going to be the Packers' main play.

"Every team arrives at a lead play, a bread-and-butter play," Lombardi once said. "It is the play that the team knows it must make go and the one opponents know they must stop. Continued success with it, of course, makes a No. 1 play because from that success stems your own team's confidence. And behind that is the basic truth that it expresses a coach as a coach and the players as a team. And they feel completely satisfied when they execute it successfully."

The sweep was known as 49 or 28 depending on the formation and which side of the field the play would go. It was simple, yet it would require hard work, preparation, discipline, execution, and organization.

In Green Bay practice would start with the play being run again and again and again. During Lombardi's first training camp he took the team to Pewaukee, Wisconsin, a week before the regular season opener against the Chicago Bears. Players on offense remember running nothing but the sweep during the first few days. Lombardi would work with each player, coming up with as many as twenty options, depending on what the opposing linebacker, safety, defensive end, or cornerback would do.

The players ran the play over and over. When practice ended, the offense would run their wind sprints out of the sweep formation. The ball would be snapped and they'd run 20 yards at a time.

It was not unusual for Lombardi to single out a player and run the play again and again with him shouting out what the player was doing wrong. Five times. Ten times. "Read the block. Drive your man," he would yell.

The players went to bed thinking about the sweep. Lombardi would throw different defenses at them. They were expected to be able to react to anything the opposition tried.

"There can never be enough emphasis on repetition. I want my players to be able to run this sweep in their sleep. If we call the sweep twenty times, I'll expect it to work twenty times...not eighteen, not nineteen. We do it often enough in practice so that no excuse can exist for screwing it up."

Left tackle Bob Skoronski, who missed the 1957 and '58 seasons because he was in the military, said in *When Pride Still Mattered*, "You're watching this day after day and it starts sinking in, becoming second nature," he said. "And after a while you say, 'I don't care what happens, we can make this thing go.'"

The play could be run to either side of the field. Usually when the ball is snapped, the guards lurch forward, trying to drive their man away to create an opening for the ball carrier. The sweep was different. When the ball was snapped, the guards would take a step back and pivot in whatever direction the play was headed. They ran parallel to the line until they reached the tackle, then they turned up field, with the back behind looking for daylight.

The play wasn't going to work unless everyone executed their blocks. The tight end, who lined three yards off tackle, had one of the key early blocks. When the ball was snapped he quickly took aim at the outside linebacker. If the linebacker moved to the inside, he was pushed that way so the running back could go to the outside. If the linebacker tried going to the outside, the end would go with him, pushing him away from the play as the back cut to the inside.

Ron Kramer became a full-time starter in 1960. By 1961 he had mastered his role on the play. If he didn't make the right play on the linebacker, the play was usually done before it got started.

"Kramer doesn't get enough credit for the blocking he did on that play," Hornung recalled. "He was so strong. Those linebackers didn't stand a chance with him."

If the play was going to the right, center Jim Ringo quickly moved in that direction and took out the left tackle that had an opening to the backfield when right guard Jerry Kramer pulled out. Thurston also pulled right as did Skoronski, the left tackle, looking to hit anyone who tried entering the backfield. Forrest Gregg, the right tackle, on the side where the play was going, was responsible for slamming into the defensive end before turning and looking to deliver a block on the middle linebacker. The back who didn't have the ball went to hit the tackle or make a follow-up block on the end.

The split end and flanker executed blocks on either the safety or cornerback, depending on the direction of the play.

When the play was executed to perfection, Kramer and Thurston had mismatches with cornerbacks and safeties. When that happened, the 5-yard plan suddenly became much bigger.

Both Taylor and Hornung were gifted enough to make the proper read. Another element to the play was the halfback option, which was suited for

Hornung, a former quarterback. Because of his ability to throw, the players in the secondary had to hesitate for a second before trying to stop the run. If they read run from the start and left the end open, Hornung would have a wide-open target.

Because of the option blocking of the tight end and the runner's ability to cut inside or outside, the sweep was really two plays in one. Three, if you add the extra dimension of the halfback option pass off the sweep action.

"Paul was just a marvelous runner," Kramer said. "He had great instincts, great feel, was smart. He just had a lot of shit going for him. He'd set it up half the time too. He didn't have the blinding speed, you know, so he would take a step this way, then come back to set up the play, or to set the block up. He did a wonderful job of doing that as we turned to go downfield."

"There is nothing spectacular about it," Lombardi once said of his sweep. "It's just a yard gainer. But on that sideline, when the sweep starts to develop, you can hear those linebackers and defensive backs yelling, 'Sweep!' Sweep!' and almost see their eyes pop as those guards turn up field after them. It's my number-one play because it requires all eleven men to play as one to make it succeed, and that's what 'team' means."

Dowler, who was the flanker throughout Lombardi's time in Green Bay, laughed as he remembered how excited Lombardi would get while diagramming the play.

"He'd be saying something like, 'Then you cut back in the alley,' and then the chalk he was pushing would break in half," Dowler recalled. "But he wouldn't pay any attention to it. The chalk would fall to the floor, but he'd keep right on going."

The Packers rushed for 1,421 yards (119-per-game average) the year before Lombardi arrived. In 1959, after spending much of training camp introducing his players to the sweep, Lombardi's Packers rushed for 1,907 yards or 158 per game—the most since the days Curly Lambeau coached. That average jumped from 158 yards per game to 178 in 1960 when Green Bay won the Western Conference and played in the NFL championship game, losing 17–13 to the Eagles.

"The concept was outstanding because we had strong running backs, and we could run the power sweep both to the strong side and to the weak side," said quarterback Bart Starr. "The Power Sweep got its name running mostly to the strong side but we could, because of the blocking capabilities of our receivers, also run it to the weak side. Because they blocked so well we were able to generate a great deal of yardage running to both sides."

Starr and the passing game became a bigger part of the offense in 1961, when the Packers averaged 168 yards per game on the ground and 5.0 per carry. Starr completed 58 percent of his passes while attempting a career-high 295 passes. He threw 16 touchdown passes—12 more than the previous season and for 2,418 yards.

The Packers won eleven of fourteen games during the regular season and then crushed the Giants in the title game, 37–0, with Starr throwing 3 touchdown passes and Hornung running for 1, in addition to kicking 3 field goals.

The sweep may have been designed with the left halfback in mind, but Taylor became a benefactor as well. Like Hornung, he had excellent timing, seizing the opportunity when he saw his opening. He often gained extra yards by dragging a linebacker or cornerback with him until some other defender helped wrestle Taylor to the ground. Taylor loved to dish out punishment almost as much as he loved gaining yards.

Taylor had his first 1,000-yard season in 1960, when he ran for 1,101 during the twelve-game season. He rushed for 1,307 yards and 15 touchdowns in 1961 when he averaged a whopping 5.4 yards per carry.

The 1962 season turned out to be the best for Taylor, who set a Packer record with 1,474 rushing yards and a league record with 19 touchdowns from scrimmage. As he had done the year before, he averaged 5.4 yards per carry. Jimmy Brown of the Cleveland Browns cast a big shadow over Taylor but not that season as Taylor was named the league's Most Valuable Player.

"Pound for pound Jimmy Taylor was one of the best football players I played with," Packers defensive end Willie Davis said.

Dowler admits almost fifty years later that neither he nor McGee were particularly strong blockers.

"We both had assignments, and I must have made a block once in a while because we were successful," he said.

The Packers averaged 175.7 yards rushing per game in 1962. They were held to less than one hundred times just three times and topped the 200-yard mark five times. They gained 160 yards or more in four other games.

"We were the only team that ran that sweep," Dowler said. "Other teams tried to copy it but they didn't have the guards who could run and get out front and get things done like Fuzzy and Jerry. Linemen today don't pull and run like those guys did."

Kramer enjoyed how involved he and Thurston were in the play because it glamorized his position, which, coincidentally, was the same position Lombardi played in college. Kramer also remembered the center, right tackle, and tight end being integral parts of the play.

"There was Ringo, who had to make an onside block and then go for the middle linebacker; he would make a call depending on what he thought he could do at that time," Kramer said. "That was a critical part of the equation: Jim getting to the middle linebacker or if Jim called to go the other way. Forrest Gregg would whack the defensive end with his right arm and then try and get on to the middle linebacker.

"That combination worked really well. Jim was smart and Forrest was a helluva blocker," Kramer continued. "He used wonderful techniques and was consistently doing the right things in the right place in the right position.

"Ron Kramer was a moose. We called him oofus. Norm Van Brocklin (Vikings coach) called him a runaway beer truck or something like that. His chore was the linebacker, and he did a hell of a job on that. Throw all those combinations together and all the pieces were there."

"The block by the tight end was the key to the whole deal," said Pat Peppler, the Packers' personnel director from 1963 through 1969. "If the tight end got the linebacker to commit to the outside, he just kept pushing him farther and farther out."

Ron Kramer had his best year in 1962, making All-Pro for the only time in his career. He had been a first-round draft pick in 1957. He had a good rookie season catching 28 passes before breaking his leg in the second-last game of the season. He missed 1958 because of military obligations and didn't report to camp until late in 1959. Out of football shape both mentally and physically, he did little to impress that year. He was inconsistent in 1960, getting into Lombardi's doghouse for running the wrong way on a pass route.

He was a talented athlete, having been both a football and basketball standout at the University of Michigan. He became a full-time starter in 1961 and by 1962 was feared throughout the league, especially by linebackers who stood in his path on the sweep.

The Packers didn't win the title in 1963, when Hornung was suspended for gambling. They failed again in 1964 when Taylor had his last 1,000-yard season. With Taylor in decline, the Packers became more of a passing team as the rushing attack lost much of its effectiveness. Ringo was traded to the Eagles after the 1963 season, and Ron Kramer was dealt to Detroit the following year.

"We were in the locker room one day talking about it and somebody asked, 'What the hell has happened to our sweep. What are we doing different,'" Jerry Kramer recalled. "Red Cochran, our backfield coach, was sitting there. He was kind of a wit, and he said, 'Hell, there ain't no secret to that. Half of it is in Philadelphia and the other half is in Detroit.'"

In its heyday, the line of Jim Ringo, Fuzzy Thurston, Jerry Kramer, Forrest Gregg, Bob Skoronski, and Ron Kramer was immoveable. These players were instrumental in making Lombardi's Power Sweep revered in the long and glorious history of the game.

CHAPTER 8

The End of Perfection

Entering the week of Thanksgiving, the Packers were sitting on top of the professional football world. They had played ten games and won all ten. There were several blowouts including a pair of 49–0 victories. The offense was averaging 30.9 points per game. The defense, which had posted three shutouts and held two other teams without an offensive touchdown, was allowing just 8.4 points.

There were two close games won against the Baltimore Colts and, of course, the 9–7 win over the Detroit Lions, courtesy of 26-yard field goal by Paul Hornung with just thirty-three seconds remaining.

Vince Lombardi preached perfection, but when he was asked about whether his team could actually win every game, his mood sometimes would turn surly. He scoffed at such a notion. Maybe he truly believed that it was impossible for a team, no matter how talented, to get enough breaks to actually win all fourteen games. He probably also thought if he did admit that going unbeaten was a possibility perhaps his players would get soft, and soft players don't go 14–0.

Lombardi would have had a hard time dealing with all the reporters and TV cameras in today's frenzied world of all-out sports coverage. The Miami Dolphins went 14–0 during the 1972 season and won three games in the postseason to finish 17–0. That perfect season attracted lots of attention, and it was the storyline heading into Super Bowl VI, but that was before ESPN, the NFL network, and the Internet supplied around-the-clock coverage.

Some of those who played for the Packers in 1962 remember idle conversation about the possibility of winning every game, but it wasn't the kind of talk that consumed them. Newspapermen, especially those who covered teams that played the Packers, raised the question about perfection through much of that season. Once Lombardi would answer that "it was highly unlikely," the topic was dropped.

Right guard Jerry Kramer remembers thinking as they went into the Thanksgiving game against the Lions that the Packers would keep right on rolling.

"I pretty much felt we were going to beat them," he said.

Kramer had reason to feel confident. The Packers were leading just about every important team category in the league.

Individually, Jim Taylor was the league's top rusher. Willie Wood and Herb Adderley ranked first and second in interceptions. This was a team full of special players accomplishing special things. Rival coaches such as Weeb Ewbank of Baltimore and Norm Van Brocklin of Minnesota insisted the Packers were beatable, but as the Packers approached December, a perfect season was not out of the question.

The Packers had received some luck in the first game against the Lions when Milt Plum threw a pass on third down in the final minute. The ball was picked off by Herb Adderley, which set up Hornung's game-winning field goal. When the Colts drove to the Packers 7-yard line in the closing minutes, the defense stiffened and Adderley batted away a pass in the end zone to snuff out the upset bid. Teams of destiny need such moments. Maybe the Packers really could win every game.

Surprisingly, in the days leading up to the Lions game, Lombardi let a television crew cover team meetings for a report about a team on the way to an unbeaten season. It was uncharacteristic for Lombardi to allow a media outlet to have such access, especially with the division title still up for grabs. It was a decision the coach would later regret.

Despite being 10–0, the Packers had their share of problems. Hornung was still hobbled by a bad knee and had played very little since hurting it in the second game against Minnesota. Tom Moore was performing admirably as his replacement, but the Golden Boy had that certain quality for performing in the clutch that not many others possessed.

Left linebacker Dan Currie also had a bad knee and wouldn't play against the Lions. His backup, Nelson Toburen, suffered a neck injury against the Colts and was also out. Starting in their place would be Ken Iman, a backup center pressed into emergency duty as a defensive player. The Packers faced another distraction when the mother of left guard Fuzzy Thurston died two days before Thanksgiving. She was scheduled to be buried the day after the game.

The Packers had been the Lions' foe in the annual Turkey Day game since 1951, which didn't sit well with Lombardi. He thought teams that traveled to Detroit had an unfair advantage and felt that the opponent should be rotated. His complaints didn't fall on deaf years. The Packers played the Lions in 1963 and after that the league began doing what Lombardi requested.

Waiting for the Packers that Thursday at Tiger Stadium was a group of angry and hungry Lions, who at 8–2 still held out hope for a division title and still harbored bad feelings for the loss that occurred in Green Bay on October 7.

The Lions lost to the New York Giants 17–14 two weeks after the game against the Packers to fall two games behind in the race to the Western Division title. While their offense had cooled considerably after scoring 119 points in the first three games, the defense carried the team. From Roger Brown and Alex Karras up front to Joe Schmidt at middle linebacker and back to the secondary where Night Train Lane and Yale Lary were among the best at their positions, the Lions didn't have any glaring weaknesses on that side of the ball.

They had allowed 140 points but only 60 in the six games after the loss to the Packers. Green Bay's defense had allowed a league-low 2,118 yards but Detroit was a close second, having given up 2,126 or 8 yards more. Both teams had held opposing teams to 129 first downs, tied for best in that category.

In recent meetings between the teams, defense set the tone. The Lions beat the Packers in the season opener the previous year, 17–13, but the Packers came back that Thanksgiving for a 17–9 win. Then there was the game that yielded a total of 16 points, played in Green Bay the first time the teams played each other in 1962. Jerry Kramer, Thurston, and the other offensive linemen usually dominated opposing defensive linemen. But Brown and Karras were a handful and had success in either sacking Starr or hurrying him into bad throws.

The Packers could seemingly score at will against most foes but totaling just 39 points in the three previous games against the team from the other side of the lake was not a good sign.

"In Detroit that week we weren't concerned about the Packers offense," said right linebacker Carl Brettschneider, who was having the best season of his nine-year career. "We knew we could hold them. We just wanted our offense to score a few more points than it did in Green Bay. We still had a chance for the title, slim and none, but we had a chance. If we won they still had to lose one of their last three games. But what was most important was we didn't want them to go undefeated. We wanted to be the team that would beat them."

Schmidt had similar feelings. There had been bad blood between the teams, and it only got worse after the last-minute loss to the Packers earlier that season.

"At the time we felt we were a better football team," he said.

While Lombardi didn't care for the game on Thanksgiving Day, Schmidt enjoyed it. The Lions had been playing a traditional holiday game since 1934. Schmidt joined the team in 1953 and quickly got used to playing a game four days after the previous Sunday and then having a long break before the next one. It also was one of the few chances in those days to play on national television.

"TV, as far as sports was concerned, was still in its infancy," Schmidt said. "People were always glued to the TV on Thanksgiving because it was a good day to watch something. The first thing you want to do is watch a little TV and then have a little dinner.

"Even today I run into people I don't even know and one of the things they talk about is the Lions on TV on Thanksgiving. They tell me that the Thanksgiving game was such a big game in their house. I think it did create a lot of NFL fans and enjoyment for many families."

On the day of the game the Lions were ready and so were more than 57,000 full-throated fans that began booing the visitors as soon as they came into view at Tiger Stadium.

From the start it appeared it would be a long day for the Packers. Karras, Brown, and defensive ends Sam Williams and Darris McCord were on top of Starr almost as soon as he received the snap from center Jim Ringo. Starr was sacked nine times for a total of 83 yards in the opening two quarters and he lost another 22 yards on a fumble when Brown stripped the ball from him, and Williams recovered on the 6 and walked in for a touchdown.

Starr was also tackled by Brown for a safety. When Taylor and Moore got a handoff they had little room to run, thrown for losses five times between them.

"I didn't have time to find anybody most of the time," Starr told reporters after the game. "There were too many people chasing me."

In addition to the points scored by the Detroit defense, Plum threw scoring passes of 33 and 27 yards to Gail Cogdill. Across the country, football fans, expecting to see the Packers continue their pursuit of the perfect season, saw instead a fired-up Lions team take a 23–0 lead by intermission.

"Detroit had a helluva defense, and Fuzzy and Jerry had a helluva time blocking their tackles," Hornung recalled.

"Poor Bart," defensive end Willie Davis said years later. "They really took it to him that day."

Years later Thurston said he and Kramer created the lookout block. As soon as Ringo snapped the ball, one of them would yell, "Look out, Bart."

The Lions eventually stretched their lead to 26–0 before the Packers finally loosened up and scored 2 fourth-quarter touchdowns. One came when Davis recovered a fumble in the end zone after Bill Quinlan, the other Packers end, intercepted a pass thrown by Plum. Taylor ended the scoring with a 4-yard run, set up when the Packers recovered a fumble at the Detroit 14.

Had the Lions not committed five turnovers, the final margin could have been worse. Starr lost 100 yards on 11 sacks and the Packers finished with a season-low 122 yards. Taylor was held to 47 yards on 13 carries as his line rarely gave him a chance to get into the open field.

The Lions gained 304 yards, including 157 on the ground.

"Our offense gave them their points," said Brettschneider, recalling the turnovers that aided the Packers.

"I remember they took some chances, gambled a little more, did some things they hadn't done before," Kramer said of the Lions. "They took the bridle off, let the mule run, and wailed our ass. They played one hell of a football game."

Following the defeat, Lombardi walked around the locker room talking gently with his players. When he met reporters, Lombardi smiled and said, "What can I do for you gentlemen? Ask and I shall answer.

"I think we will be a better football team for having lost this one. That business about an undefeated season was a lot of bunk. Nobody in his right mind could have expected it. The loss had to come sometime, but I honestly didn't think it would come today. We weren't flat. I thought we were ready to go. But you can't always sense these things. We were completely overpowered in the first half."

Lombardi was asked if things would have been different had Hornung played.

"I don't think that having Hornung would have made any difference," Lombardi said. "The way Detroit was charged up I don't think Paul could have done any more than the rest of the guys."

Before he ended his session with the media the coach said this: "It's funny. We were overpowered, the winning streak is broken and we're not invincible, but we're still in first place and that's what counts."

Lions coach George Wilson also had a lot to say, especially about what he thought had happened when the teams played in October.

"We didn't think the Packers should have won that first game at Green Bay," he told reporters. "They were lucky. Then, we've been reading all these magazine stories about how great they are. Our kids were mad. I could sense all week they were going to give me something extra today. I didn't have to say a word to them today."

Wilson admitted that his team had not played well in previous games because they had been looking forward to the rematch with Green Bay.

"I'm afraid we looked right past a couple of other teams. I hope we can stay this high for our last three games," he said.

Going back to the end of the previous season, the Packers had won eighteen straight games, including exhibitions, before their streak ended so abruptly on that cold day in Detroit. Instead of wrapping up the division title, their lead was down to one game over the Lions.

Hornung's recall of the game was of Lombardi letting that television crew into team meetings in the days leading up to the game.

"I think Vince was pissed at himself for that and blamed himself for the loss," Hornung said.

Kramer remembers he and his teammates being more upset for losing so convincingly rather than for having the winning streak stopped.

"I don't have much of a memory for thinking about trying to go unbeaten," he said. "We were disappointed with the loss, disappointed with getting our butts kicked. Fuzzy's mother had passed away a couple days before the game, and maybe there had been concern with those types of things.

"We were certainly disappointed to lose the game, but it wasn't like we thought we were going to have a perfect season and that this was going to destroy our memory forever."

The Packers had a 10–1 record with two games remaining against the Rams and one against San Francisco, the two worst teams in the Western Division. The Lions had games left with the Colts, Vikings, and Bears. The Lions whipped the Packers and gained payback for the 9–7 loss in Green Bay, but the season was fourteen games long. The Packers were still in control of their destiny, still leading the division, still on a path that would give them a chance to successfully defend their championship.

Lombardi wouldn't allow them to wallow in self-pity. As he said after the game, this would serve as a learning experience and would help his team in the long run.

The Lions were euphoric. They were back in the race but they also—at least back then—thought they may have proved they were a better football team with how thoroughly they had defeated the Packers in the nationally televised game. But as Brettschneider and Schmidt look back, they realize that a championship is not won with one victory over a fourteen-game season.

"It was very satisfying, and that Thanksgiving Day game was important to us," Brettschneider said. "But we did blow that game against the Giants. The Packers kept winning, so you have to give them credit for that. They have ten guys in the Hall of Fame plus their coach. They were a good team and they weren't easy to beat, even though we did beat them on Thanksgiving Day."

The Packers finished 13–1 and went on to beat the Giants. The Lions won their next two games, but lost to the Bears 3–0 in the final game of the season and completed the season 11–3, two games in back of the Packers. They had a superb defense but the offense wasn't consistent.

There are certainly times Schmidt has thought about the game in Green Bay, wondering what would have happened if Plum would have handed off on that third-down play rather than thrown the interception.

"We lost three games by a total of 8 points," said Schmidt, who later coached the Lions from 1967–72. "That was always a source of discomfort, especially for a defensive football team. Again, who knows, but had we won that first game maybe things might have turned out different, maybe things might have turned out to our advantage. It's hard to say. Who knows? It's hard to project that."

With the passage of time, Schmidt has allowed himself to give due credit to the Packers. He played on NFL championship teams in Detroit in 1953 and '57 and understands it's the entire body of work that makes a champion.

"Satisfaction is only when you win and win totally, so as a result you have to give those guys credit," he said of the 1962 Packers. "They had such a well-balanced, great football team. They were very well coached. It did give us some stature that we did beat them and we played them in a very close game. The game on Thanksgiving was a game of some significance, but as they went forward they maintained their winning posture and wound up being the better football team.

"They have to be considered one of the best in the era, certainly. I was lucky to play during that time, lucky to play against such good football players, and I always feel blessed that, as a young man, I had the opportunity to play when I did.

"And after all these years those Green Bay guys, I have a lot of admiration for them. Vince (Lombardi) was always very, very kind to me, so as a result I have a little soft spot in my heart for those guys."

CHAPTER 9

Another Division Title

When the Packers returned to Green Bay following the 26–14 loss to the Lions that ended the chance of an unbeaten season, the story in the *Green Bay Press-Gazette* the next day was almost as if Vince Lombardi had written it himself.

The lead to the report, written by sports editor Art Daley read:

> *The inevitable has happened. The Packers lost. Detroit did it. The score was 26–14. Thirty million people via national television, plus 57,598 saw the game in Tiger Stadium Thanksgiving Day. This was no disgrace. The proud world champions lost to two forces—the Lions, who are perennial runners-up to the champs, and pressure built up by an 18-game winning streak, not to mention 10 straight league victories. The monkey is off the Pack's back now. They are still in control of the Western Division title chase, with a one game lead on Detroit and three to go. The Bays are 10–1, the Lions 9–2.*

Bud Lea's lead in the *Milwaukee Sentinel* was more to the point.

A hungry band of Lions feasted on the Packers instead of turkey on this Thanksgiving Day.

The mighty Packers, unbeaten in their last 18 games (including preseason affairs) were practically devoured, 26–14. Why, it was hardly a struggle.

How could it happen? The answer was simple. Green Bay found the Detroit defense a slab of concrete.

Just imagine if that game had been played in today's world of around-the-clock sports coverage where every game is critiqued as if it's the Super Bowl.

How would the Packers of 1962 have been treated in such an environment? Maybe the national media would have jumped on the Lions bandwagon, saying Detroit was the real class of the Western Division, that had it not been for Milt Plum's ill-advised pass in the first game, the Lions would have been the team positioning itself for the Western Division title, not Green Bay.

When asked something that irked him, Lombardi would reply something like this: "That's a stupid question, mister." And then ESPN would have run the sound bite over and over.

Luckily for Lombardi and his team, the media coverage was vastly different than it is today. Daley's story in the hometown paper was tame and looked at the positive side.

Most important to the Packers heading into the final three games was that they were still in control of the division. The Packers had a game remaining with San Francisco, which had played them tough for more than a half in Milwaukee, but also two with the Los Angeles Rams, who would finish with the worst record in the NFL that season.

Naturally, the Packers were disappointed with losing on national television but they took Lombardi's cue: the focus was on repeating as world champions. The Packers were still in charge of their own fate. Learn from the defeat and move on.

"I can honestly say when we lost that game we still basically had the championship won," defensive end Willie Davis recalled almost fifty years after that loss to Detroit. "I would say to you that maybe something went away as far as the opportunity to win every game, but something went away as far as lifting some of the pressure.

"It got to be where pressure was definitely a factor. There was pressure on the defense, pressure on the offense—pressure even on some of the individual spots. It was a tough game in Detroit, but it was only one game and we were still in first place."

While Lombardi didn't have to deal with a nasty media, he did receive a letter from a Japanese Packers fan living in Los Angeles who wrote the coach after the loss to Detroit and before the Packers' next game against the Los Angeles Rams.

Lombardi was so amused that he shared it with the *Press-Gazette*.

I don't think any team can lose anything by teaching fundamentals of such skills of Japanese wrestling while professional futbol is a mixture of brute force and balancing skills. Judo and karate tactics will be really helpful to a quarterback when he face with bigger and heavier linemen, especially in red dog situations. If Bart Starr had such experience it would be lot easier for him to evade or outmaneuver such behemoths like Alex Karras or Roger Brown or Brettschneider. Otherwise straight force can't do anything against such monsters. Such skills would have helped your team last Thursday when ferociousness of Lions could be evened by such skills as well as similar ferociousness from your side.

Lombardi chuckled as he read the latter and agreed his team needed to be more ferocious but didn't need to be taught karate and judo.

His job was to make sure they perfected the art of football, beginning with the game against the Rams.

Bouncing back

Packers 41, Rams 10
Milwaukee County Stadium
December 2

Ten days after losing to the Lions, the Packers returned to their championship form with a 41–10 win over the Los Angeles Rams, who entered the game with just one win and one tie in its eleven previous games.

Paul Hornung played for the first time in nearly two months since suffering a knee injury against Minnesota. The Golden Boy scored a touchdown on a 30-yard pass and set up another with a 35-yard reception. He also carried the ball nine times for 27 yards before leaving the game after re-injuring his knee.

His touchdown reception was the first score of the day as the Packers never trailed. He ran his assigned route and wasn't picked up by a defender.

"I sure was lonesome on that one," he told reporters after the game.

He also talked about whether he had any concern about the knee holding up.

"You never know what's going to happen," he said. "It wasn't until the first time I cut back that I knew everything was all right."

Jim Taylor, who had been held in check in the two previous games against Baltimore and Detroit, gained 71 yards on 16 carries, his best outing ever against the Rams defense. He scored twice on short runs, his 16th and 17th touchdowns of the season.

The previous day Taylor became a father for the first time when James Charles Taylor was born in Green Bay.

"That took some of the pressure off me," he told reporters when asked about his first born. "That pretty well ended the worry and strain."

The Packers' air attack was superb as Starr completed 15 of 20 passes for

260 yards. In addition to the 30-yard strike to Hornung he also threw a scoring pass of 4 yards to burly tight end Ron Kramer. He would have had a third, but a touchdown pass to split end Max McGee was called back because of a penalty.

The Green Bay defense had a solid showing as well, sacking Roman Gabriel four times for a total of 48 yards in losses. Tackle Henry Jordan had a highlight with the first interception of his career.

"It was my first interception in fourteen years of football," said Jordan, who counted his days in high school and college. "Then, I didn't know what to do with it after I got it. Once a lineman, always a lineman, I guess."

The mood was light in the locker room after the game. Lombardi was pleased with how his team came back after the loss on national TV to Detroit.

"I thought they responded real well. I expected them to come back," said Lombardi, who seemed surprised his team scored so many points.

"I never expect to get that many points," he said. "I don't worry about points. I just want to win."

Starr, who was sacked eleven times in Detroit, was taken down five times by the Rams, which may have had something to do with Lombardi appearing to scold his linemen on the sidelines a couple of times during the game.

When asked about that he smiled and said, "That's between me and them."

He referred to the remaining two games as an endurance contest. The NFL was in its second season of a fourteen-game schedule, two more than previous.

The Lions stayed a game behind with a 21–14 win over Baltimore. Elsewhere in the league the Giants wrapped up another Eastern Division crown with a 26–24 win against the Bears, guaranteeing them of a return to the championship game, which would be held in New York on December 30.

The story in the *Press-Gazette* said coach Allie Sherman walked around the Giants locker room hugging and kissing his players. Although it wasn't mentioned in the story it was well known in New York that the Giants wanted the Packers to be their opponent in the title game. They had some revenge to take care of for the 37–0 whipping the Packers gave them in the 1961 championship game.

Tight end Ron Kramer scores on a pass from Bart Starr in the final minute of the second quarter of a 41–10 rout of the Los Angeles Rams.

"Let me tell you this is a much better club than most people think," Sherman said. "In fact, we were wondering about it ourselves. But now we know it is a great club."

Lombardi tried to hide his irritation when one writer asked him about what appeared to be another rematch with the Giants and whether the 1963 Packers would be better than the current team.

"We are not thinking of the playoffs, we are still trying to earn a place in it," he said. "As far as next year, there's no point in even discussing it."

Quite a comeback

Packers 31, 49ers 21
Kezar Stadium, San Francisco
December 2

The toughest games to win are sometimes those in which a team with everything on the line plays a team that doesn't have anything to play for except pride.

That appeared to be the case when the Packers traveled to the West Coast for their second meeting with the 49ers. Back in October the Packers won the first game between the teams, 31–13, although they trailed early and had their hands full for more than a half.

This time the Packers needed a win to clinch at least a tie for their third Western Division title; the 49ers had a 6–6 record, thanks to a three-game winning streak. They were loose and looking to make the Western Division race a little more interesting, which for more than a half, they did.

Led by quarterback John Brodie, the 49ers took an early 14–3 lead, and after Tom Moore scored on a 5-yard run to pull the Packers within 14–10, the 49ers scored before the end of the half when Brodie connected on a 5-yard pass with Clyde Conner for a 21–10 lead. Brodie, a young gunslinger who had helped beat the Packers a year earlier, continued to show he was one of the better quarterbacks in the league. He completed 20 of 31 passes for 269 yards and 2 touchdowns.

Earlier in the day the Lions had already defeated Minnesota 37–23, which meant a loss would drop the Packers into a tie for the division lead with one game remaining. But that wasn't going to happen as they roared back onto the field in the second half.

Starr directed a twelve-play, 83-yard drive at the start of the third quarter that culminated with Moore exploding for a 32-yard score on a quick opener that cut the 49ers' leads to 4 at 21–17.

Hornung started at halfback but after 4 carries he was replaced by Moore, the effects of a knee injury and the long layoff between starts showing. Moore wound up with 56 yards on 13 carries, showing once again that he was a capable replacement.

The Packers took the lead for good early in the fourth quarter when Taylor scored from 2 yards out for a 24–21 lead.

Brodie took San Francisco back down the field, driving inside the Green Bay 11 with eight minutes remaining. Facing fourth down they could have tried a field goal that would have tied the game, but coach Red Hickey elected to go for a first down. Brodie tried a pass to Clyde Conner who got a hand on it in the end zone, but couldn't make the catch.

"If I had thrown the ball just a little softer so Clyde could have had time to get both hands on it, it's 6 points," Brodie said.

After the game Hickey defended his decision to try and take the lead.

"I felt obliged to the league to try and win this game. A tie would have been just as good as a win for the Packers, and it wouldn't have been fair to the Lions if we had settled for a tie," Hickey said. "You can't say we didn't try knocking them off for the Lions."

Defensive end Dave Hanner ended another 49ers drive with an interception, and then Ken Iman, still filling in for Dan Currie at left linebacker, recovered a fumble deep in San Francisco territory.

The Packers completed their scoring when Starr tossed a 4-yard touchdown pass to Ron Kramer that put the finishing touches on the comeback and elevated Green Bay to a 12–1 record and at least a share of a third division title just four years after they compiled a 1–10–1 record.

"We played a fine game," Lombardi said. "They showed great poise in coming back in the second half. We don't fold."

Hickey had a lot of praise for how the Packers played in the second half.

"They certainly showed the poise of champions coming from behind like that," he said. "I don't want to take anything away from them."

Lombardi talked about how the season was beginning to grind on Taylor, who had been averaging more than 5 yards a carry most of the season. Against the 49ers he was given the ball twenty-four times and gained 79 yards, or 3.3 yards per carry. Taylor was leading the league in rushing and touchdowns, but Lombardi mentioned he was down to 204 pounds, more than a 10-pound loss since the beginning of the season.

Nobody knew it at the time but Taylor was struggling with hepatitis, which wouldn't be diagnosed until after the championship game.

"He's a tough son of a gun," Packers defensive coordinator Phil Bengtson said. "Jim's always banging you and he never gets hurt."

Lombardi talked about how the length of the season had been taking a toll on the Packers because their season started before other teams because as champions they had to play the college all-stars.

"We have not been playing as well in the past few games as we did earlier," Lombardi said. "You have to remember we were in camp two weeks longer than any of the others because of the all-star game."

Undisputed champions

Packers 20, Rams 17
Los Angeles Coliseum
December 16

Carroll Dale, an eighth-round draft choice, was nearing the end of his third season with the Rams when they played the Packers twice during the final three weeks of the 1962 season.

Dale was turning into a fine receiver but was frustrated playing on a losing team. He can remember a longing feeling to be with a winner, especially when the Rams played Green Bay. He obviously didn't know it at the time, but Dale would become a Packer before the 1965 season.

"When you have a couple of years of frustration, just to imagine being on a contender was like a dream," he said. "And in my case not only was the team attractive to me, but the town was too. I'm a small-town boy and if somebody would have come in and said you can pick where you want to play, I would have picked Green Bay because they had all of the attractive qualities.

"I like winners and small cities so when it happened it was like a dream come true."

When the Packers and Rams played to close out the 1962 regular season, the West Coast team had a league-worst 1–11–1 season; the Packers had a league-best 12–1 mark. Green Bay was looking to win the undisputed Western Division title; the Rams couldn't wait to end a disastrous season.

As was the case against the 49ers, a win wasn't going to be handed to the Packers. They never trailed but were pushed to the brink before escaping with a 20–17 win.

During the first quarter they heard on the loudspeaker at the Coliseum that the Bears defeated the Lions 3–0, assuring the Packers of an undisputed championship. The players shook hands on the sidelines, congratulated themselves on returning to the title game, but they still wanted to finish with a win. They did because of the performance of some of their key players.

Ron Kramer scored the game's first points on a 45-yard halfback option thrown by Tom Moore, the backup who had started more than half the games because of Paul Hornung's injured knee.

Taylor, who had been held to less than 100 yards for three straight games, rushed for 156 yards and scored on a 28-yard run. He finished the season as the league's leader in rushing (1,474 yard), touchdowns (19), and scoring (114 points).

Hornung came off the bench to score on an 83-yard pass from Starr that gave the Packers a 20–7 lead early in the fourth quarter.

Dale scored on a 15-yard pass from halfback Jon Arnett that pulled the Rams to 20–17, but that's how it ended.

The Packers finished with 427 yards, but 2 fumbles thwarted scoring opportunities.

When it was over there was very little celebration in the locker room. The Packers were tired and knew their job wasn't finished. They would try to repeat as champions in two weeks against the Giants at Yankee Stadium.

Taylor talked about how the team played hard after hearing the score of the Lions game.

"I think we played 100 percent," he said. "We knew we had to put out because the minute you let up at all, somebody gets hurt. We need everybody for the playoff."

Lombardi said, "We're a tired ball club, a very tired ball club."

Asked why his locker room lacked emotion, Lombardi said, "When I say we're tired I don't mean physically. I don't believe a young man gets physically tired. But we are mentally tired. This wasn't a season. It was an endurance contest."

Lombardi also had to deal with questions about Hornung, who, according to a report, was unhappy because he had played so little since injuring his knee in early October.

"Why don't you ask Paul about it?" the coach said. "I did and he laughed."

When reporters approached the Golden Boy he shrugged it off.

"I'd be a nut to want to be traded from this team."

Looking back Hornung said, "I got hurt and it was hard not playing as much as I did because I hadn't been hurt like that before."

That season was a long one for Hornung, who had been the league scoring champion the three previous years. Hornung appeared in nine games, although he played very little in the last three. He scored 74 points, 102 fewer than the 176 he scored in 1960 when he set a league record.

Nobody knew it at the time but the long touchdown pass he hauled in from Starr would be his last points until 1964. In the spring of 1963, Hornung and Lions tackle Alex Karras would be suspended indefinitely for gambling and associating with gamblers.

In Green Bay Hornung was betting heavily, sometimes as much as $500 a game. He bet on the Packers, to win, and also on college games. Some of his teammates would make a wager through him from time to time. The FBI began investigating Hornung, Karras, and several other players who may have associated with gamblers. Hornung eventually was called to New York for a meeting with NFL commissioner Pete Rozelle, who wanted names from Hornung. The Green Bay halfback admitted his wrongdoing but would not point the finger at others. Hornung also refused to take a lie detector test.

In addition to punishing Hornung and Karras, Rozelle fined five other Lions players $2,000 each for placing $50 bets on the Packers to win the NFL title game against New York. The Packers covered the 6 ½-point spread, which meant the fined players were out $1,950 since the Packers won the game, 16–7.

During his press conference Rozelle said, "There is no evidence that any NFL player has given less than his best in playing any game. There is no evidence that any player has ever bet against his own team. There is no information that any NFL player has ever sold information to gamblers. There is clear evidence that some NFL players knowingly carried on undesirable associations which, in some instances, led to their betting on their own team to win and/or other National Football League games."

"I took one for the team, no question about it," Hornung said years later. "I was wrong and the commissioner did the right thing. The only thing I regret is nobody (other than Karras) was treated like I was. There were a couple guys on the 49ers, a couple guys on the Rams, guys in Kansas City. There was more than one guy betting. Pete Rozelle got one guy named Hornung and made an example out of him because he wanted to scare the shit out of everyone else."

Hornung returned in 1964 but the layoff and a pinched nerve in his neck took a toll on him. He did have a couple of stellar performances in 1965, scoring 5 touchdowns in a late-season win over Baltimore and later rushing for 105 yards in a 23–12 win over Cleveland in the 1965 championship game.

Hornung sat on the bench for most of the 1966 season. The Packers placed him and 10 other players on a list for a special draft for the New Orleans Saints, the NFL's newest expansion team. The Saints picked Hornung, who eventually retired without playing one game.

As a team, the Packers finished first in points scored (415) and in points allowed (148). They had a winning margin of 19.1 points per game. In addition to Taylor, other league leaders were Starr in completion percentage (62.5) and Wood in interceptions (9). The Packers led the league with 31 interceptions and in forced turnovers with 50.

"That was just an outstanding football team, especially on defense," Dale remembered. "Herb Adderley of course was extremely quick and fast, and Willie Wood just had wonderful instincts for the football. He always seemed to be in the right place at the right time.

"What makes great defensive backs are great defensive lines and linebackers that can put pressure on opposing quarterbacks, and the Packers always seemed able to do that. That's why you call it team. Conversely what makes great quarterbacks and receivers is a great offensive line. When the quarterback has time to throw, it makes it virtually impossible to cover receivers."

Two weeks later the Packers would go on to beat the Giants in a violent, hard-hitting contest to win their second straight title. Lombardi had his sights set on three straight in 1963 but the Bears ruined that, beating the Packers twice on their way to an 11–1–2 record. Hornung, of course, was suspended for the season because of the betting scandal. The Packers finished 11–2–1.

Dale came onboard in 1965 when the Packers won their third championship under Lombardi. Dale was a key receiver when the team repeated in 1966 and '67 to finally give Lombardi the three straight championships he so dearly coveted.

"It took them awhile to get it," Dale said with a chuckle, "and then they got me and got it done."

The Packers' third straight Western Division title in 1962 was just another indication of how far the team had come since the disastrous 1958 season. In four

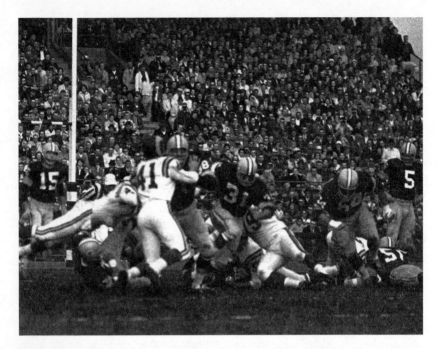

Jim Taylor (31) shows the running style that earned him the league's
Most Valuable Player award. Teammates Paul Hornung (5), Jerry Kramer (64),
and Bart Starr (15) lend a hand.

seasons with Lombardi the Packers had won 75 percent of their regular-season
games, winning thirty-nine against just thirteen losses. Their record during the
1961 and '62 seasons was a combined 26–4.

"It was just an incredible two seasons," said Packers flanker Boyd Dowler.

It showed not only in the win column but in the postseason awards. Fourteen
Packers were named either first or second team to at least one of the various All-
Pro teams: offensive linemen Jim Ringo, Jerry Kramer and Forrest Gregg; tight
end Ron Kramer; quarterback Bart Starr; fullback Jim Taylor; defensive linemen
Willie Davis and Henry Jordan; linebackers Ray Nitschke, Bill Forester, and Dan
Currie; cornerback Herb Adderley; and safety Willie Wood.

Six of the players were consensus first-teams: Jerry Kramer, Ringo, Gregg, Forester, Currie, and Taylor.

Making the Pro Bowl were both Kramers, Ron and Jerry; Forrest Gregg; Bill Forester; Henry Jordan; Max McGee; Jim Ringo; Starr; Taylor; and Moore, the one-time backup who became a key figure after Hornung got hurt.

Taylor was named the league's Most Valuable Player. A few weeks before the MVP announcement the *Press-Gazette* ran quotes from defensive players who had faced Taylor during the past two years.

Giants linebacker Sam Huff: "When you get him you gotta sit on him or he'll keep moving. You gotta pile on him a little to keep him down."

49ers linebacker Bob Harrison: "One time Taylor saw me waiting for him and he ran right at me. I planted my feet wide apart to be as solid as possible but he hit me so hard that he knocked me right into the air. I went right off my feet and landed on my back. That never happened to me before in my life. Then he picked me up."

Lombardi had this to say about his leading ground gainer: "Taylor may not be as big as some fullbacks but he has balance and determination. He is hard to knock off his feet and he fights for every yard."

CHAPTER 10

The Players

ow special were the Green Bay Packers in 1962?

The offense scored a league-best 415 points, the defense limited opponents to a league-low 148 points.

Six players were consensus All-Pro picks. Eight others were honored as All-Pro players by at least one of the four associations that chose teams that season. Nine players were voted to the Pro Bowl.

Jim Taylor led the NFL in rushing and scoring and was named the league's MVP. Willie Wood's 9 interceptions were the best in the league as was Bart Starr's passing percentage of 62.5.

It's amazing that ten players on a roster of thirty-six would eventually be voted into the Pro Football Hall of Fame. Some of the players on the 1962 team were either traded or had retired by the time the Packers won their fifth NFL championship and the second of their two Super Bowl wins at the end of the 1967 season. Amazingly, six of the Hall of Fame players and eight others were part of all five championship teams.

Vince Lombardi was the architect of that dynasty, winning the first of his five league titles in 1961, just three seasons after the Packers finished with the worst record in the NFL.

His team nearly achieved perfection in 1962, winning twenty of twenty-one games, including six exhibitions and the 16–7 triumph of the New York Giants in the championship game.

Lombardi, who died of colon cancer in 1970, also was elected to the Hall.

The following are the players and coaches on that almost-perfect team:

OFFENSIVE STARTERS

RIGHT END MAX MCGEE. Tied for team lead in catches (49) and was first in receiving yards (820). Had 3 touchdown receptions.
CAREER: Drafted in fifth round by Packers in 1954. Was in the service for two years before returning in 1957. Played twelve seasons and finished with 345 catches for 6,345 yards and 50 touchdowns. Also ran for 1 touchdown. Was one of Lombardi's favorites because of his sense of humor. During one training camp when Lombardi held up a ball, telling his team it was a football, McGee famously replied, "Hold on coach, you're going too fast." Had one of his greatest games in Super Bowl I, catching 2 touchdown passes and finishing with 7 catches for 138 yards in the 35–10 win over Kansas City. Died in 2007.

LEFT END BOYD DOWLER. Was a four-year veteran who tied McGee for the team lead with 49 receptions. Totaled 724 yards and had 2 touchdown passes. Was the team's primary punter and averaged 43.1 yards per kick, sixth-best in the league.
CAREER: Drafted in 1959, he played eleven seasons for the Packers and was a player-assistant coach for the Washington Redskins in 1971. Finished with 474 catches for 7,270 yards and 40 touchdowns. Was the NFL Rookie of the Year in 1959. Caught 2 touchdown passes in the 1967 NFL championship game against Dallas and had a touchdown reception in the Super Bowl II win over Oakland two weeks later. Was selected to the Pro Bowl twice.

TIGHT END RON KRAMER: Had arguably his best season with 37 catches for 555 yards and 7 touchdowns. Also was a key blocker especially on Lombardi's Power Sweep. Was selected to three All-Pro teams and to the Pro Bowl.

CAREER: Caught two scoring passes in the 1961 championship game. Drafted in the first round in 1957 by the Packers. Missed the 1958 season and then returned and played from 1959 through 1964 before being traded to Detroit, where he played his final three seasons. Had 229 career receptions for 3,272 yards and 16 touchdowns. Died in 2010.

CENTER JIM RINGO. Speed and mobility were the key traits in his role as a blocker in Lombardi's sweep. Made the Pro Bowl and was a consensus All-Pro pick.

CAREER: Seventh-round draft choice by Packers in 1953. Played first eleven seasons with the team before being traded to Philadelphia, where he played four more seasons. Made the Pro Bowl for the tenth time in his final season in 1967. Was a consensus All-Pro with the Packers from 1959 through 1963. "Ringo was a great player and very effective on the sweep," said Pat Peppler, the Packers' former player personnel director. Elected to the Pro Football Hall of Fame in 1981. Died in 2007.

LEFT GUARD FUZZY THURSTON. The native of Altoona, Wisconsin, was a key component of the sweep, which was the most effective play for the Packers. His blocking helped Jim Taylor rush for 1,474 yards. Was named to three All-Pro teams. "Thurston was an outstanding downfield blocker on the sweep," Peppler said. "Jerry Kramer was stronger and more athletic, but Fuzzy was more effective as a blocker in the open field."

CAREER: Drafted in the fifth round by the Eagles in 1956. Signed as a free agent with Baltimore in 1958 and earned a championship ring as the Colts beat the Giants in the famous Sudden Death game, 23–17. Traded to the Packers in 1958, where he remained until retiring following the 1967 season. Was a consensus All–Pro pick in 1961.

LEFT TACKLE BOB SKORONSKI. Alternated with Norm Masters during the 1962 season. Became the full-time starter in 1963.

CAREER: Drafted by the Packers in the fifth round in 1956. Missed the next two seasons and returned from 1959 through 1968. Was selected to the Pro Bowl in 1966 and was one of the offensive captains for much of his career. "When people talk about our line, Bob Skoronski gets left out, and I don't like that," said Bart Starr, the Packers Hall of Fame quarterback. "I'm very, very disappointed he's not in the Hall of Fame. When I look at the people in the Hall of Fame, and they deserve to be there, but Bob Skoronski is not there? To me it's just shameful. This guy was a brilliant offensive tackle."

LEFT TACKLE NORM MASTERS: Shared left tackle with Skoronski during the Packers' first two championships in 1961 and 1962.

CAREER: Originally drafted by the Chicago Cardinals in 1956. Signed by the Packers in 1957 and retired in 1964. When Jerry Kramer broke his leg in 1961, Masters started at right tackle when Forrest Gregg moved to right guard.

RIGHT GUARD JERRY KRAMER: Missed the 1961 NFL championship game because of a broken foot. Came back in 1962 and was a consensus All-Pro. Took over kicking duties when Paul Hornung was injured. Made 38 of 39 extra-point attempts and 9 of 11 field-goal tries during regular season. Booted 3 field goals in the 16–7 win over Giants in 1962 title game. "When Jerry swung his foot it looked like the ball was going to explode," said Packers defensive end Willie Davis. "But he did a great job for us, especially in that championship game."

CAREER: Drafted by the Packers in the fourth round in 1958. Played through the 1968 season. Twice was a consensus All-Pro and was selected to at least one of the All-Pro first teams five times. Also played in three Pro Bowls, including 1962. Named to the NFL's All-Decade team in the 1960s and to the NFL's Fifty-year Anniversary team. Best known for making the key block in the famous Ice Bowl game, which enabled Bart Starr to score the winning touchdown in the 21–17 win over Dallas in the 1967 NFL championship game.

RIGHT TACKLE FORREST GREGG. Lombardi called him one of the most intelligent players he ever coached. Was a consensus All-Pro and a Pro Bowl selection.

CAREER: Second-round pick by the Packers in 1956. Was a consensus All-Pro pick four times. Played in the Pro Bowl nine times. Also earned a Super Bowl ring with Dallas in 1970. Gregg showed his versatility in 1961 when Kramer was injured and Gregg moved to right guard where he spent half a season. Later was a head coach for the Cleveland Browns and Cincinnati Bengals, guiding the Bengals to a Super Bowl appearance in 1981. Was the Packers' head coach from 1984 through 1987. Elected to the Pro Football Hall of Fame in 1977. Named to the All-Decade team in the 1960s and to the Seventy-fifth NFL Anniversary team.

QUARTERBACK BART STARR. Efficient leader of the offense. Completed 62.5 percent of his passes while throwing for 2,438 yards and 12 touchdown passes. Tossed just 9 interceptions. Named to three All-Pro teams and to the Pro Bowl.

CAREER: Drafted in the seventeenth round by Green Bay in 1956. Did not assume full-time duties as quarterback until midway through the 1960 season when the Packers reached the NFL title game for the first time under Lombardi. Played through the 1971 season. Was named to four Pro Bowls and was the NFL's MVP in 1966 and the MVP in the first two Super Bowls. In six NFL championship games and two Super Bowls, Starr threw 13 touchdown passes and had just 2 picked off in 189 attempts. Scored the winning touchdown against Dallas in the 1967 NFL title game known as "The Ice Bowl." "After Lombardi came, Bart became one of the great leaders in the history of the game," halfback Paul Hornung said. Inducted into the Hall of Fame in 1977. Coached the Packers from 1975 through 1983.

HALFBACK PAUL HORNUNG: Injuries limited him to nine regular season games in 1962 although he started the championship game against the Giants. Rushed for 219 yards and 5 touchdowns and also caught 2 touchdown passes, booted 6 field goals, and 14 extra points.

CAREER: First-round draft pick in 1957 after winning the Heisman Trophy in 1956 during his senior season at Notre Dame. Became a full-time halfback

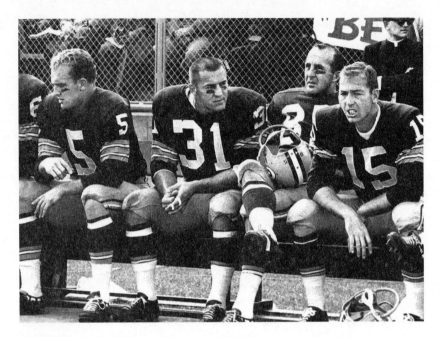

From left, Paul Hornung (5), Jim Taylor (31), Max McGee (85), and
Bart Starr (15) take a rest during a 49–0 victory over the Chicago Bears on
September 30, 1962.

when Lombardi was hired as coach in 1959. Was the NFL's MVP in 1961, a
year after he scored 176 points in twelve games, a record that stood until 2006
when San Diego's LaDainian Tomlinson scored 186 points on 31 touchdowns.
Was suspended in 1963 for gambling and returned to play for the Packers three
more seasons. Was at his best in big games. He scored 19 points and rushed
for 89 yards in the 1961 championship game and rushed for 105 yards and 1
touchdown in the 23–12 win over Cleveland in the 1965 title game. Inducted
into the Hall of Fame in 1986.

FULLBACK JIM TAYLOR. Named the NFL's MVP in 1962 after running for 1,474
yards and 19 touchdowns during the regular season. Scored the Packers' only

touchdown in their 16–7 win over New York in the championship game. "Jim Brown led the league in rushing every year he played except in 1962 when Jim Taylor did it," said Willie Davis. "Taylor was always looking for someone to hit. He was one tough guy."

CAREER: Packers took him in the second round of the 1958 draft. Became a starter after Lombardi arrived, rushing for 1,000 or more yards from 1960 through 1964. Five-time Pro Bowl selection. Played ten seasons, including one with New Orleans. Rushed for 8,597 yards. Inducted into the Hall of Fame in 1976.

DEFENSE

END WILLIE DAVIS: Anchored a defense that forced 50 turnovers and held opponents to 148 points in fourteen games. He scored 1 touchdown on a fumble recovery during that championship season.

CAREER: Originally a seventeenth-round pick by Cleveland in 1958, was traded to the Packers in 1960. Played ten seasons and on all five of Lombardi's championship teams. Sacks weren't kept during that era, but researchers who have looked at film estimate that Davis had at least 140 sacks during his ten seasons in Green Bay. "Tackles had a hard time blocking him because he was so quick off the ball," Hornung said. Was a consensus All-Pro four times and played in five Pro Bowls. Named to the 1960s All-Decade team. Inducted into the Hall of Fame in 1981.

TACKLE HENRY JORDAN. Along with Davis harassed opposing quarterbacks. Threw 31 interceptions during the 1962 season. Was first-team All-Pro on two teams.

CAREER: Played first two seasons with Cleveland before Packers acquired him in a trade in 1959. One of the first key moves made by Lombardi as he began to build a defense that would lead the franchise to five titles and two Super Bowl wins. Was a consensus All-Pro twice and played in four Pro bowls during a career that ended in 1969. Died in 1977 when he was forty-two. Was elected to the Hall of Fame in 1995.

TACKLE DAVE HANNER. At thirty-two, was the oldest starter for the Packers on the 1962 team. Popular among his teammates and in the Green Bay community. Even though he didn't retire until 1964, the Packers held a "Hawg Hanner Day" during the season.

CAREER: A fifth-round pick by Green Bay in 1952. Was a two-time Pro Bowl selection. Died in 2008.

END BILL QUINLAN. Recovered 1 fumble and had an interception during the regular season.

CAREER: Drafted in third round by Cleveland in 1956. Traded to the Packers in 1959. Was traded to Philadelphia following the 1962 season and played with the Eagles one season. Also played one season with Detroit and one with Washington before retiring following the 1965 season.

LEFT LINEBACKER DAN CURRIE. Tough guy who was effective against the run. Returned an interception 30 yards in the championship game. Was a consensus All-Pro selection.

CAREER: Third-round draft choice in 1958 by the Packers. Traded after the 1964 season to the Rams. Had 11 career interceptions. Was on at least two of the All-Pro first teams three straight years (1961–63).

MIDDLE LINEBACKER RAY NITSCHKE: The 1962 season was his first as a full-time starter, launching a string of successful seasons that would land him in the Hall of Fame in 1978. Was All-Pro and earned MVP in the 16–7 title-game win over the Giants after recovering 2 fumbles and deflecting a pass that led to an interception. Had 4 interceptions and 4 fumble recoveries during the regular season.

CAREER: Third-round draft choice in 1958. Was a consensus All-Pro in 1966. Named to the NFL's Fiftieth- and Seventy-fifth-year All-Anniversary teams. Made 25 interceptions during his fifteen-year career. Died in 1998.

RIGHT LINEBACKER BILL FORESTER: Recovered 2 fumbles while making at least one All-Pro team for the third consecutive season.

CAREER: Originally a third-round pick by the Packers in 1953. Spent entire career with the Packers, retiring after the 1963 season. Was named to the Pro Bowl four times and earned first-team All-Pro recognition on at least one of the teams four times. Died in 2007.

LEFT CORNERBACK HERB ADDERLEY: Was elected first team All-Pro on two teams after making 7 interceptions in 1962. Also was the team's main kick returner. He had a 103-yard return for a touchdown in a 17–13 win over the Colts. "Adderley was a great athlete and cornerback," said former Colts running back Tom Matte.

CAREER: A first-round pick, Adderley was moved from offense to defense out of necessity during his rookie season. Played nine seasons with Green Bay and three with Dallas. Finished with 48 career interceptions. Was a consensus All-

Herb Adderley gallops 103 yards for a touchdown on a kickoff during the Packers' victory over the Baltimore Colts on November 18, 1962.

Pro twice and voted to the Pro Bowl team five times. Inducted into the Hall of Fame in 1980.

RIGHT CORNERBACK JESSE WHITTENTON. Part of a strong secondary that had 31 interceptions. He had 3 and also recovered 2 fumbles.
CAREER: Played first two seasons with the Rams before Packers acquired him in 1958. Retired after the 1964 season. Was a first-team All-Pro on two teams in 1961. Played in two Pro Bowls. Had 24 career interceptions.

SAFETY HANK GREMMINGER. Made 5 interceptions and recovered 1 fumble in 1962.
CAREER: Third-round pick by Green Bay in 1956. Played on three championship teams before finishing his career with Rams in 1966. Died in 2001.

FREE SAFETY WILLIE WOOD: Two years after making the team as an undrafted free agent, Wood led the NFL with 9 interceptions in 1962. Made the Pro Bowl for the first time.
CAREER: Signed by Packers in 1960. Played in eight Pro Bowls and was consensus All-Pro twice. Broke open Super Bowl I with a 50-yard interception returned during the Packers' 35–10 win over Kansas City. Elected to Hall of Fame in 1989. "That secondary with Wood and Adderley back there was just incredible," the Colts' Matte said.

RESERVES

WIDE RECEIVER GARY BARNES. Appeared in thirteen games, mostly on special teams. Did not catch a pass.
CAREER: Drafted by the Packers in the third round in 1962, his only season with the team. Played with three other teams and caught 41 passes during a five-year career.

GUARD ED BLAINE. A second-round draft pick in 1962, he played mostly on special teams.

CAREER: Traded to Philadelphia in 1963, where he played his final four seasons.

FLANKER LEW CARPENTER: A backup who caught 7 passes during the regular season.

CAREER: Spent three seasons with Detroit and two with Cleveland before Packers acquired him in 1959. He played on two championship teams before retiring after the 1964 season. Later served as an assistant coach for the Packers. Died in 2010

DEFENSIVE TACKLE RON GASSERT: A fourth-round pick in 1962 who appeared in ten games in his only season in the NFL.

FULLBACK EARL GROS. As a rookie rushed for 155 yards and 2 touchdowns in a backup role.

CAREER: The team's first-round pick in 1962, he was traded to Philadelphia in 1964. Rushed for 3,157 yards during a nine-year career with four different teams.

CENTER KEN IMAN. Third-year player, who played at tiny Southeast Missouri State. Started two games at left linebacker when Currie was injured late during the season.

CAREER: Iman was traded to the Rams, where he eventually played in 140 straight games before retiring following the 1974 season. He was an offensive line coach for ten seasons with the Philadelphia Eagles. Died in 2010.

END GARY KNAFELC. Was Lombardi's starting tight end in 1959 and 1960. Played primarily on special teams in 1962.

CAREER: Was a second-round draft choice of the Chicago Cardinals in 1954 and played one game before being signed by the Packers. Had his best season in 1955 when he caught 40 passes and scored 8 touchdowns. Played one season in San Francisco before retiring in 1963. For his career, caught 154 passes and scored 23 touchdowns. Later served as the Packers' public address announcer.

DEFENSIVE TACKLE RON KOSTELNIK: Backed up veteran Dave Hanner and played on special teams.

CAREER: Second-round draft pick in 1961 and became a full-time starter in 1964. Was with the Packers for all five NFL championships and two Super Bowl wins under Lombardi. Played one season with the Colts in 1969. Recovered 7 fumbles during his nine-year career. Died in 1993.

HALFBACK TOM MOORE: Was the Packers' second leading rusher with 377 yards, filling in for Paul Hornung. Also scored 7 touchdowns. Was selected to the Pro Bowl for the only time in his career. "Tom was a good football player and did a nice job for us that year with Hornung being injured," said flanker Boyd Dowler.

CAREER: Packers' first-round pick in 1960. Played on three championship teams before he was traded to the Rams following the 1965 season. Played one season

Willie Wood (24) talks to Elijah Pitts (22) during a game with the Chicago Bears. Others on the sideline include, from left, Tom Moore (25), Ken Iman (53), Willie Davis (87), Bill Forester (71), and Gary Knafelc (84).

in Los Angeles and one in Atlanta. Rushed for 658 yards for the Packers in 1963. Ran for 2,445 yards during his eight-year pro career and scored 31 touchdowns, including 27 with the Packers.

RUNNING BACK ELIJAH PITTS: Rushed for 110 yards and played on special teams in his second season.

CAREER: Thirteenth-round draft pick in 1961. Was part of all five NFL teams and two Super Bowl wins with Vince Lombardi. Scored 35 career touchdowns. Played eleven seasons in the NFL including ten with the Packers. When Pitts was worried he may not make the team in 1961, Paul Hornung gave him words of encouragement, telling Pitts, "You'll be here longer than I will." Pitts scored 2 touchdowns in the first Super Bowl after scoring 1 two weeks earlier in the 34–27 win over Dallas in the 1966 NFL championship game. Died in 1998.

QUARTERBACK JOHN ROACH: Threw 12 passes in a backup role to Bart Starr.

CAREER: Spent the 1961 through 1963 seasons in Green Bay before playing one season with the Cowboys in 1964. Was with the Chicago/St. Louis Cardinals for three seasons before joining Packers.

DEFENSIVE BACK JOHN SYMANK: After intercepting 5 passes in 1961, Symank played mostly on special teams in 1962, although he replaced the final two quarters in the 1962 championship game after Willie Wood was ejected.

CAREER: Drafted in the twenty-third round by Green Bay in 1957. He had 19 interceptions and recovered 11 fumbles during a seven-year career.

LINEBACKER NELSON TOBUREN. Appeared in ten games, mostly on special teams.

CAREER: Was a fourteenth-round draft pick by Lombardi in 1961. Played two seasons in the NFL, both in Green Bay. Died in 2002.

DEFENSIVE BACK HOWIE WILLIAMS. Signed as a free agent and appeared in one game.

CAREER: Returned to Packers in 1963 and played in seven games. Also played in seven games with San Francisco. Wound up playing six more seasons with the Oakland Raiders in the AFL. Played against the Packers in Super Bowl II.

ASSISTANT COACHES

PHIL BENGTSON, DEFENSIVE COORDINATOR, 1959–67. The only member of Lombardi's original staff who stayed with him throughout his nine seasons with the Packers. Bengtson ran the defense, which was the best in the league in 1962, yielding just 148 points while posting 3 shutouts. Before his arrival in Green Bay, Bengtson was an assistant for seven seasons with the San Francisco 49ers. When Lombardi stepped down from coaching, Bengtson had the unenviable task of succeeding the man who had guided the Packers to five NFL titles and victories in the first two Super Bowls. Bengtson compiled a 20–21–1 record as the Packers head coach following the 1970 season. His 1969 team had an 8–6 record—the only time that one of the four Lombardi assistants who would become an NFL head coach had a winning record. He had a 1–4 record as interim head coach with New England in 1972. He died in 1994.

NORB HECKER, DEFENSIVE BACKS COACH, 1959–65. Hecker was a defensive back with the Los Angeles Rams from 1951 through 1953; with Toronto of the Canadian Football League in 1954; and with the Washington Redskins from 1955 through 1957. He had 28 career interceptions. With the Redskins, he was one of the founders of the NFL Players Association in 1956. Hecker served as head coach of the Atlanta Falcons from 1968 through the first three games in 1970, when he was fired. He was defensive coordinator for the New York Giants from 1969 though 1971 and then went into college coaching. He came back as an NFL assistant with the 49ers in 1979 and eventually moved into the front office until retiring in 1991. During his time in San Francisco, the team won four Super Bowl titles. He died in 2004.

BILL AUSTIN, OFFENSIVE LINE COACH, 1959–64. Lombardi knew him from New York, where Austin was a lineman in 1949–50 and from 1953–57. He eventually was head coach for the Pittsburgh Steelers from 1966 through 1968 and rejoined Lombardi as an assistant with Washington. When Lombardi died just before the start of the 1970 season, Austin served as interim coach for the entire season and then retired from football.

RED COCHRAN, BACKFIELD COACH 1959–66. Played three years as running back/defensive back with the Chicago Cardinals and served as an assistant with the Lions before joining Lombardi's staff. He was a Packers assistant from 1971 through 1974 and then scouted for the team from 1975 until his death in 2004.

TOM FEARS, OFFENSIVE ENDS COACH, 1962–65. Before becoming a coach, he was a superb offensive end, establishing the NFL single-season record for receptions with 77 in 1949 and in 1950 with 84. He also set a single-game record with 18 catches against the Packers in 1950. He caught 400 passes during his nine-year career, which eventually landed him in the Hall of Fame. He was the first head coach of the New Orleans Saints, fired midway through his fourth season after failing to put up a winning record. He died in 2000.

CHAPTER 11

The Essence of Lombardi

Vince Lombardi came to Green Bay in the winter of 1959 knowing that this would be his one shot to prove to the world that he could be a head coach. Not a competent one, but a great one.

He was a man of faith and courage who was totally dedicated to the game of football. He preached discipline and dedication. He sought commitment and excellence.

By the end of 1962 everyone knew Lombardi and the Green Bay Packers, the team that resided in the smallest city of the fourteen teams in the National Football League. The team that lost ten games in 1958 had a winning record in Lombardi's first season and was playing for a National Football League championship in his second.

They didn't win but Lombardi made sure his players learned from that defeat, and he promised them they would never lose another championship game while they were together. He was, of course, right.

Beginning in 1961 the Packers won the first of five NFL championships under Lombardi during a seven-year period. The last two of those seven seasons culminated with the playing of the first two Super Bowls, the champion from the NFL against the champion from the rival American Football League. The Packers won both in convincing fashion, and Lombardi and his players became legends.

There have been other teams that had great runs but not the sustained greatness the Lombardi Packers had. The Miami Dolphins played in three straight Super Bowls, winning two, the first of which resulted in the perfect 1972 season. The Dallas Cowboys from 1992–95 won three Super Bowls but again fell short of the Packers.

The one team that did come close was the Pittsburgh Steelers, who during a six-year stretch played in four Super Bowls and won all four. Nine players from that era are in the Hall of Fame.

Ten players from Lombardi's championship teams are in the Hall of Fame, and they are names that resonate with football fans, especially those in Wisconsin, who remember those teams.

Quarterback Bart Starr, right tackle Forrest Gregg, defensive end Willie Davis, defensive tackle Henry Jordan, middle linebacker Ray Nitschke, cornerback Herb Adderley, and safety Willie Wood played on all five champion teams.

Fullback Jim Taylor and halfback Paul Hornung played on four of the teams, and center Jim Ringo on two. Had it not been for Lombardi, it's a safe bet that most, if not all, would not have had the type of careers that allow them to live forever in Canton.

Davis was a backup with the Cleveland Browns when Lombardi obtained him in a trade before the 1960 season. Jordan also was a reserve for Cleveland when Lombardi acquired him before the 1959 season.

"I left Cleveland after having played in a playoff game my first year and go to Green Bay to play in six championship games and walk away winning five of them," Davis said, not including the Super Bowl victories. "So there's no question that worked out well for me."

"If it hadn't been for him I probably would have quit football," said Hornung, who led the league in scoring during his first three seasons with Lombardi. "I needed a sense of direction and purpose in my life at that time, and that's what he gave me."

"There's no question that none of this would have happened had it not been for Vince Lombardi," said Jerry Kramer, Lombardi's right guard during all of those championship seasons and the man who made the block that enabled Bart Starr to score the winning touchdown over Dallas in the 1967 NFL championship game, better known as the "Ice Bowl," the game played on New Year's Eve at Lambeau Field when the temperature was minus 13 and the field was as hard and slippery as a hockey rink.

The final drive, perhaps more than any other during his nine seasons in Green Bay, highlighted everything that Lombardi had taught his players: commitment to excellence; teamwork; never quit.

Trailing 17–14 in a game they once led 14–0, the Packers began a drive with 5 minutes, 32 seconds remaining and marched 68 yards in 12 plays. After halfback Donny Anderson slipped two times in a row trying to score from the 1, Starr called a timeout and suggested a wedge between center Jerry Bowman and Kramer, who is not in the Hall of Fame but was selected to the NFL's Fifty-year Anniversary team.

"Run it and let's get the hell out of here," Lombardi told his quarterback.

In the huddle everyone thought fullback Chuck Mercein was getting the ball, but Starr decided to keep it himself and wedged himself across the goal line to complete one of the greatest drives in NFL history.

When the Packers easily beat the Oakland Raiders 33–14 two weeks later in the second Super Bowl, Lombardi's place in history as perhaps the game's greatest coach was firmly secured.

The longer Lombardi stayed in Green Bay, the more he became regarded as a tyrant, a madman, by those who weren't around him every day. Writers sometimes wrote articles that portrayed him as a cruel, soulless person.

After making his block in the Ice Bowl, Kramer, while interviewed moments after the game, said this about Lombardi: "Many things have been said about

Coach, and he is not understood by those who quote him. The players understand. This is one beautiful man."

Lombardi was demanding because he expected perfection. He could appear heartless at times when he chewed out a player so hard in front of teammates that the player victim would tell himself that he was through, he didn't want to play for that crazy coach anymore. Almost instinctively Lombardi would come and rub the player's shoulder or mess up his hair—his way of saying everything is all right, you're still my guy, we're in this together.

"There's no one I ever played for that was more motivational than Coach Lombardi," Davis said.

The Packers compiled an 89–29–4 record in nine seasons under Lombardi. Toss in a 9–1 postseason record, and his overall record was 98–30–4. He retired after the second Super Bowl and spent a season away from the sidelines, serving solely as the Packers' general manager.

Lombardi became antsy. He missed coaching, missed being on the field. The Washington Redskins made him an offer in 1969 that he couldn't refuse. They asked him to coach and also gave him a small percentage of the team. He asked for and received permission from the Packers' executive committee to leave for Washington.

The Redskins weren't as bad as the 1958 Packers, but they weren't winners either. They hadn't had a winning season in the twelve before Lombardi arrived, twice finishing with just one victory. Lombardi inherited a team that had won five of fourteen games in 1968.

The old spark was back. He worked the Redskins as hard as he worked the Packers. Quarterback Sonny Jurgensen lacked direction but had a strong arm. By the end of 1969 the Redskins were a formidable outfit, finishing with a 7–5–2 record.

There were high hopes for the Redskins in 1970, but Lombardi was stricken with colon cancer and he didn't last long, dying on September 3.

Counting playoffs he compiled a 105–35–6 record. The success he had in Green Bay became the stuff of legend. His players who are still living, still work on "Lombardi time," still follow the principles taught to them so many years ago by a one-time assistant coach who became one of the greatest coaches in the history of football.

"When people today go on the Internet to find out what football was all about, there's so much respect for what Vince Lombardi and the Green Bay Packers did for the National Football League," said Tom Matte, a running back for the Colts who played against the Lombardi-coached Packers for seven seasons. "They just won so many damn championships."

CHAPTER 12

The '62 Packers or '72 Dolphins?

When the 1962 season ended and the Packers had secured their second straight championship, the accomplishments of that dynamic team coached by Vince Lombardi led to discussions that the team was on the short list of greatest teams in NFL history.

Fourteen wins in fifteen games. First in points scored and fewest allowed. Three shutouts and two other games when the defense didn't allow the opposing offense to reach the end zone. Fourteen players honored on various All-Pro teams; nine selected to play in the Pro Bowl; fullback Jim Taylor was the league's Most Valuable player.

The Packers won five games by 30 or more points and three others by at least 17. The offense averaged 29.6 points per game and the defense allowed 10.6.

Thirteen years earlier the Philadelphia Eagles won the NFL's Eastern Division with an 11–1 record and won the championship game with a 14–0 win over the Los Angeles Rams. The Eagles averaged 30.2 points per game while allowing 11.0. They posted 2 shutouts and allowed just 1 field goal in three other games. That team, led by running back Steve Van Buren and noseguard Chuck Bednarik, won three games by 30 or more points. Seven of their eleven regular-season wins were by 21 or more points.

While the numbers posted by the Eagles and Packers in their respective seasons of domination are similar, it's hard to make any strong comparisons because the game had changed significantly. Most players weren't wearing facemasks in 1948, and many of the Eagles played both ways.

In the facemask and platoon era, the Packers had no equals. The Bears dethroned them as NFL champions in 1963, posting a 11–1–2 record before beating the Giants 14–10 in the championship game. Chicago had a superb defense, allowing 144 points or 4 fewer than the 1962 Packers and holding the opposition to 7 or fewer points in eight games. But the offense averaged just 21.5 points per game. That Bears team simply wasn't as dominating as the Packers had been in 1962.

The 1966 Packers won twelve of fourteen games, beat Dallas 34–27 at the Cotton Bowl for the NFL title, and on January 15, 1967, won the first Super Bowl with a 35–10 win over the Kansas City Chiefs, champions of the American Football Conference. The defense had many of the same players as 1962 and at times dominated games. The offense, though, was not as potent, scoring 335 points or 80 points less.

During the early years of the NFL there had been teams that didn't lose a game but suffered at least one tie. One of those teams was the 1929 Green Bay Packers, which went 12–0–1 to give coach Curly Lambeau his first of six championships. But that team won the title by virtue of its record. The NFL was not divided into divisions until 1933 when the first championship game was played. The Bears finished the regular season unbeaten and untied in 1934 and again in 1942, but ended both seasons with losses in the league title game.

The one team that did finish unbeaten and untied throughout the regular seasons was the Cleveland Browns in 1948. The Browns were playing in the short-lived All-America Football Conference, and although the Browns and some other teams from that league joined the NFL, the NFL does not acknowledge records from the AAFC.

So as the years went by the 1962 Packers appeared to be the best NFL team at least in the era of the foruteen-game schedule, which began in 1961. That distinction lasted until 1972 when the Miami Dolphins went 14–0 and then won three playoff games, including Super Bowl VI to finish 17–0, the first team to finish with a perfect season with a playoff system in place.

The Dolphins were coached by Don Shula, who had coached against Lombardi's teams when he was defensive coordinator of the Detroit Lions and later the head coach of the Baltimore Colts.

Shula was coach of the Colts when they were 18-point favorites in Super Bowl III but lost to quarterback Joe Namath and the New York Jets, 16–7. After one more season in Baltimore, he was hired by Miami and performed a Lombardi-like turnaround of the organization.

The Dolphins joined the AFL in 1966 but compiled a 15–39–2 record in their first four seasons. Shula came in and led the team to a 10–4 record and a second-place finish in the AFC East. The next year he took the team to the Super Bowl, losing to Dallas 24–3. His 1972 team made history, and the 1973 team repeated as Super Bowl winners, beating the Minnesota Vikings 24–7.

There were many similarities between the '62 Packers and '72 Dolphins. Both posted 3 shutouts. Overall, the Packers gave up 148 points compared to 171 by the Dolphins, who allowed just 20 more yards (3,297) than the 1962 Packers.

On offense the Dolphins scored 385 points, or 30 fewer than the Packers and weren't as explosive, although they did beat New England 52–0. Despite not scoring as much, the 1972 Dolphins gained 5,036 yards of total offense, more than 200 more than Green Bay, which totaled 4,791.

Both teams had exceptionally strong running attacks. Jim Taylor rushed for 1,474 yards and 19 touchdowns for the 1962 Packers, which led the league in rushing with 2,460 yards. Miami also led the NFL in rushing in its year of perfection, running for an astounding 2,960 yards, or 211 per game.

Miami's rushing leader was Larry Csonka, who, like Taylor, ran over people. He rushed for 1,117 yards but just 6 touchdowns. He may have had more had it not been for Mercury Morris, who reached the end zone 12 times and rushed for an even 1,000 yards.

Bart Starr was a smart, efficient quarterback for the Packers. Bob Griese was comparable to Starr, but he suffered a dislocated ankle in the fifth game and was replaced by thirty-eight-year-old Earl Morrall, who held onto the job until Griese replaced him in the American Football Conference championship game against Pittsburgh, which the Dolphins won 21–17.

Both teams had to come back late for a victory. The Packers needed a late interception and then a field goal with thirty-three seconds left to defeat Detroit 9–7. Miami's close call was a 16–14 win over the Minnesota Vikings. The Dolphins trailed 14–6 going into the fourth quarter. A field goal by Garo Yepremian sliced the deficit to 5 at 14–9, and then Griese threw a 4-yard touchdown pass to tight end Jim Mandich in the final minute as the Dolphins escaped with a win and improved to 4–0.

"Perfection ends any arguments," Csonka once said when asked if his Dolphins team was the greatest of all time.

Pat Peppler served as the Packers' player personnel director from 1963–72 before becoming the Dolphins' director of pro scouting before the 1972 season began. When asked to compare the teams, he paused for several seconds before answering.

"That's a tough one," said Peppler, who also worked for the Atlanta Falcons, Houston Oilers, and New Orleans Saints before retiring in 1985. "The Packers did have ten Hall of Famers on that team, and that's saying a lot. But the Dolphins did win them all, something the Packers didn't do."

The Packers had five offensive players who made the Hall of Fame—center Jim Ringo, right tackle Forrest Gregg, halfback Paul Hornung, Starr and Taylor. Their five defensive players on that team who made it to Canton were defensive end Willie Davis, tackle Henry Jordan, middle linebacker Ray Nitschke, cornerback Herb Adderley, and safety Willie Wood.

Six members of the 1972 Dolphins are Hall of Famers; Csonka; Griese;

center Jim Langer; right guard Larry Little; wide receiver Paul Warfield; and middle linebacker Nick Buoniconti.

Lombardi and Shula are also in the Hall.

"Csonka was a great, great fullback, maybe even stronger than Taylor, and that's saying a lot," Peppler said. "Buoniconti was an excellent linebacker, but I don't think he was in the class of Nitschke. Bart Starr was quarterback of five championship teams.

"I think the Packers had better cornerbacks in Herb Adderley and Jesse Whittenton. The Dolphins were known as the no-name defense, and they were good but they didn't have the reputation the Packers defense had."

Hornung brought a different perspective when asked whether the Packers were better than the Dolphins.

"Bob Martin, a good friend of mine who is no longer with us, was the most respected bookmaker in his day as far as making the line," said Hornung, who was suspended during the 1963 season for betting on NFL games. "He made the line every Monday for years; nobody would bet until Bob Martin would come out with the line.

"I once asked him about that Dolphin team that went undefeated. I once asked if our team when we were great played the Dolphins on a neutral field what the line would be. He said, 'I'd make you guys eight-point favorites.'

"I think we would have kicked the shit out of them. You ask anyone who saw that team. They would tell you the Packers were better. Buonoconti was a hell of a player, but can you imagine him trying to come to the outside and getting involved in our sweep and Ron Kramer coming down on him at 265 pounds? Kramer would have killed him. It wouldn't have even been close. We had ten Hall of Famers on that team plus some other guys who were All-Pro players. We had a great team."

Boyd Dowler, the flanker throughout Lombardi's run as coach of the Packers, was an assistant coach with the Washington Redskins in 1972. They lost to the Dolphins in the Super Bowl, 14–7. The Redskins' only touchdown was when

The 1962 defense shut down opposing running games and also forced turnovers. Could the likes of Dan Currie (58), Henry Jordan (74), Ray Nitschke (66), and Willie Davis (87) shut down the Dolphins?

Yepremian picked up a blocked field goal and attempted a pass that was picked off by Washington's Mike Bass and returned 49 yards for a touchdown.

"The Dolphins won all of their games but they were not an overwhelming team; there was nothing unusual about them," Dowler said. "They ran the ball really well, but I don't think they could have done that well against our defense. I'll tell you one thing: our '62 team was much better than the Redskins. Paul's right. I think we would have beat the Dolphins without any trouble."

Marv Fleming joined the Packers in 1963 and was their starting tight end in the first two Super Bowls. He was with the Dolphins during their perfect season, starting but splitting time with Mandich. Following the Dolphins' Super Bowl win he was asked by reporters to compare that team with those that won titles with the Packers.

"We never accomplished a perfect season in Green Bay," he said. "That's why this is a better team."

Fleming eventually changed his mind. In *Lombardi and Me* a book Hornung wrote with Billy Reed in 2004, Fleming talked about the coaching styles of the coaches who helped him earn a total of four Super Bowl rings.

"People always ask me about the difference between Lombardi and Shula," said Fleming, an eleventh-round draft pick who played his first seven seasons with the Packers and the last five with Miami.

"Well, Lombardi was a coach for life. Once you play for him, you can leave and go anywhere. Shula was a coach of football. He knew how to produce a good team. But if Lombardi's Packers champions had ever played Shula's Dolphins champions, the Packers would have won."

The Dolphins were perfect, but the Packers have more players in the Hall of Fame. The Packers think they were better; the Dolphins, as Csonka said, claim overall greatness because they are the only National Football League team to go through an entire season and the playoffs winning every game.

"I'd love to play them, would love to be part of that," said Jerry Kramer, the right guard on the 1962 Packers. "Put me down, I think I can still get down in my stance. Our focus was never to go undefeated. Our focus was to win three straight championships, which we did."

CHAPTER 13

The Statistics

THE 1962 SEASON

SEPTEMBER 16:	Packers 34, Minnesota Vikings 7 at City Stadium
SEPTEMBER 23:	Packers 17, St. Louis Cardinals 0 at Milwaukee County Stadium
SEPTEMBER 30:	Packers 49, Chicago Bears 0 at City Stadium
OCTOBER 7:	Packers 9, Detroit Lions 7 at City Stadium
OCTOBER 14:	Packers 48, Minnesota Vikings 21 at Metropolitan Stadium, Bloomington, Minnesota
OCTOBER 21:	Packers 31, San Francisco 49ers 13 at Milwaukee County Stadium
OCTOBER 28:	Packers 17, Baltimore Colts 6 at Memorial Stadium, Baltimore, Maryland
NOVEMBER 4:	Packers 38, Bears 7 at Wrigley Field, Chicago, Illinois
NOVEMBER 11:	Packers 49, Eagles 0 at Franklin Field, Philadelphia, Pennsylvannia
NOVEMBER 18:	Packers 17, Baltimore Colts 13 at City Stadium
NOVEMBER 22:	Detroit Lions 26, Packers 14 at Tiger Stadium, Detroit, Michigan
DECEMBER 2:	Packers 41, Los Angeles Rams 10 at Milwaukee County Stadium
DECEMBER 9:	Packers 31, San Francisco 49ers 21 at Kezar Stadium, San Francisco, California
DECEMBER 16:	Packers 20, Los Angeles Rams 17 at Memorial Coliseum, Los Angeles, California
DECEMBER 30:	Packers 16, New York Giants 7 at Yankee Stadium, New York, New York

Bottom row, from left: Elijah Pitts, Ed Blaine, Earl Gros, Gary Barnes, Ron Gassert, Oscar Donahue, Ron Kostelnik. Second row, from left: Willie Wood, John Symank, Hank Gremminger, Dan Currie, Herb Adderley, Nelson Toburen, John Roach, Forrest Gregg. Third row, from left: Jim Ringo, Bart Starr, Gary Knafelc, Jerry Kramer, Fuzzy Thurston, Jesse Whittenton, Lew Carpenter, Tom Moore. Fourth row, from left: Equipment manager Dad Braisher, Bob Skoronski, Ray Nitschke, Ken Iman, Willie Davis, Henry Jordan, trainer Bud Jorgensen. Top row, from left: Bill Quinlan, Norm Masters, Boyd Dowler, Jim Taylor, Ron Kramer, Bill Forester, Dave Hanner, Paul Hornung. Missing from the picture: Max McGee.

Game by Game
GAME 1:
Green Bay 34, Minnesota 7

TEAM STATS

	MIN	GB
First downs	14	15
Rush-yards-TDs	29–129–0	37–185–3
Comp-Att-Yd-TD-INT	11–23–100–1–5	8–16–149–1–0
Sacked-yards	6–52	3–26
Net pass yards	48	123
Total yards	177	308
Fumbles-lost	2–2	2–1
Turnovers	7	1
Penalties-yards	2–10	9–75

	1	2	3	4	FINAL
Minnesota Vikings (0–1)	0	0	0	7	7
Green Bay Packers (1–0)	14	3	10	7	34

SCORING

FIRST QUARTER

GB—Paul Hornung 6 run (Paul Hornung kick)
GB—Paul Hornung 7 run (Paul Hornung kick)

SECOND QUARTER

GB—Paul Hornung 10 field goal

THIRD QUARTER

GB—Paul Hornung 45 field goal
GB—Ron Kramer 18 pass from Bart Starr (Paul Hornung kick)

FOURTH QUARTER

GB—Paul Hornung 37 run (Paul Hornung kick)
MIN—Jerry Reichow 17 pass from Fran Tarkenton (Mike Mercer kick)

INDIVIDUAL STATS

Passing MIN—Fran Tarkenton 11–23–100–1–5. GB—Bart Starr 7–14–108–1–0; Paul Hornung 1–1–41–0–0; John Roach 0–1–0–0–0.

Rushing MIN—Fran Tarkenton 3–21; Bill Brown 2–18; Hugh McElhenny 5–38; Doug Mayberry 7–27; Bobby Reed 4–24; Tommy Mason 8–1. GB—Paul Hornung 10–67–3; Jim Taylor 17–75; Bart Starr 1–9; Earl Gros 5–14; Tom Moore 3–12; Elijah Pitts 1–8.

Receiving MIN—Bill Brown 2–31; Jerry Reichow 4–47–1; Hugh McElhenny 1–4; Bobby Reed 2–1; Steve Stonebreaker 1–10; Tommy Mason 1–7. GB—Boyd Dowler 3–95; Paul Hornung 2–2; Max McGee 2–34; Ron Kramer 1–18–1.

GAME 2:
Green Bay 17, St. Louis 0

TEAM STATS

	STL	GB
First downs	11	20
Rush-yards-TDs	18–16–0	37–171–1
Comp-Att-Yd-TD-INT	17–33–156–0–2	15–27–181–1–2
Sacked-yards	5–41	2–18
Net pass yards	115	163
Total yards	131	334
Fumbles-lost	4–3	2–2
Turnovers	5	4
Penalties-yards	2–39	5–54

	1	2	3	4	FINAL
ST. LOUIS CARDINALS (1–1)	0	0	0	0	0
GREEN BAY PACKERS (2–0)	0	3	7	7	17

SCORING

SECOND QUARTER
GB—Paul Hornung 13 field goal

THIRD QUARTER
GB—Paul Hornung 3 run (Paul Hornung kick)

FOURTH QUARTER
GB—Max McGee 19 pass from Bart Starr (Paul Hornung kick)

INDIVIDUAL STATS

Passing STL—Sam Etcheverry 15–30–124–0–2; John David Crow 2–3–32–0–0. GB—Bart Starr 14–26–173–1–2; Paul Hornung 1–1–8–0–0.

Rushing STL—Sam Etcheverry 2–0; John David Crow 9–9; Joe Childress 0–1; Mal Hammack 6–7. GB—Jim Taylor 23–122; Bart Starr 1–11; Paul Hornung 11–34–1; Earl Gros 1–5; Tom Moore 1–(–1).

Receiving STL—Bobby Joe Conrad 7–76; Taz Anderson 4–48; John David Crow 2–8; Joe Childress 2–17; Mal Hammack 1–2; Sonny Randle 1–5. GB—Jim Taylor 4–40; Boyd Dowler 5–82; Max McGee 2–33–1; Ron Kramer 4–26.

GAME 3:
Green Bay 49, Chicago 0

TEAM STATS

	CHI	GB
First downs	7	21
Rush-yards-TDs	28–85–0	42–244–5
Comp-Att-Yd-TD-INT	7–20–132–0–5	10–13–165–1–1
Sacked-yards	5–41	0–0

Net pass yards	91	165
Total yards	176	409
Fumbles-lost	1–0	2–0
Turnovers	5	1
Penalties-yards	3–31	2–26

	1	2	3	4	FINAL
CHICAGO BEARS (2–1)	0	0	0	0	0
GREEN BAY PACKERS (3–0)	0	14	21	14	49

SCORING

SECOND QUARTER
GB—Jim Taylor 1 run (Paul Hornung kick)
GB—Ron Kramer 54 pass from Bart Starr (Paul Hornung kick)

THIRD QUARTER
GB—Jim Taylor 3 run (Paul Hornung kick)
GB—Elijah Pitts 26 run (Paul Hornung kick)
GB—Jim Taylor 11 run (Paul Hornung kick)

FOURTH QUARTER
GB—Bart Starr 5 run (Paul Hornung kick)
GB—Herb Adderley 50 interception return (Paul Hornung kick)

INDIVIDUAL STATS

Passing CHI—Billy Wade 7–18–132–0–3; Rudy Bukich 0–2–0–0–0. GB—Bart Starr 9–12–154–1–1; John Roach 1–1–11–0–0.

Rushing CHI—Joe Marconi 11–46; Billy Wade 2–(–1); Ronnie Bull 8–31; Johnny Morris 1–4; Billy Martin 2–2; Rick Casares 4–3. GB—Jim Taylor 17–126–3; Elijah Pitts 9–64–1; Bart Starr 1–5–1; Tom Moore 8–22; Paul Hornung 2–14; Earl Gros 5–13.

Receiving CHI—Joe Marconi 2–76; John Adams 1–24; Johnny Morris 2–12; Mike Ditka 1–12; Billy Martin 1–8. GB—Jim Taylor 1–(–1); Elijah Pitts 2–40; Boyd Dowler 5–57; Ron Kramer 1–54–1; Max McGee 1–15.

GAME 4:
Green Bay 9, Detroit 7

TEAM STATS

	DET	GB
First downs	12	20
Rush-yards-TDs	27–107–1	34–129–0
Comp-Att-Yd-TD-INT	11–26–107–0–1	18–28–198–0–2
Sacked-yards	2–15	1–8
Net pass yards	92	190
Total yards	199	319
Fumbles-lost	0–0	2–2
Turnovers	1	4
Penalties-yards	3–47	6–67

	1	2	3	4	FINAL
Detroit Lions (3–1)	0	7	0	0	7
Green Bay Packers (4–0)	3	0	3	3	9

SCORING

FIRST QUARTER
GB—Paul Hornung 13 field goal

SECOND QUARTER
DET—Dan Lewis 6 run (Wayne H. Walker kick)

THIRD QUARTER
GB—Paul Hornung 15 field goal

FOURTH QUARTER
GB—Paul Hornung 26 field goal

INDIVIDUAL STATS

Passing DET—Milt Plum 11–26–107–0–1. GB—Bart Starr 18–26–198–0–0; Paul Hornung 0–1–0–0–1; Tom Moore 0–1–0–0–1.

Rushing DET—Milt Plum 7–58; Dan Lewis 12–30–1; Nick Pietrosante 8–19. GB—Jim Taylor 20–95; Bart Starr 1–4; Paul Hornung 10–37; Tom Moore 1–(–1); Ron Kramer 1–(–4); Earl Gros 1–(–2).

Receiving DET—Dan Lewis 3–13; Jim Gibbons 3–41; Pat Studstill 2–32; Terry Barr 2–12; Gail Cogdill 1–9. GB—Jim Taylor 3–25; Max McGee 5–69; Paul Hornung 2–10; Boyd Dowler 3–45; Tom Moore 3–23; Ron Kramer 2–26.

GAME 5:
Green Bay 48, Minnesota 21

TEAM STATS

	GB	MIN
First downs	29	15
Rush-yards-TDs	42–209–3	19–46–1
Comp-Att-Yd-TD-INT	20–29–297–3–0	18–29–288–2–3
Sacked-yards	0–0	3–28
Net pass yards	297	260
Total yards	506	306
Fumbles-lost	3–1	0–0
Turnovers	1	3
Penalties-yards	8–67	4–29

	1	2	3	4	FINAL
GREEN BAY PACKERS (5–0)	10	17	7	14	48
MINNESOTA VIKINGS (0–5)	0	7	0	14	21

SCORING

FIRST QUARTER
GB—Paul Hornung 3 run (Paul Hornung kick)
GB—Jerry Kramer 14 field goal

SECOND QUARTER
GB—Max McGee 15 pass from Bart Starr (Jerry Kramer kick)
GB—Jerry Kramer 35 field goal
GB—Max McGee 55 pass from Bart Starr (Jerry Kramer kick)
MIN—Steve Stonebreaker 19 pass from Fran Tarkenton (Jim Christopherson kick)

THIRD QUARTER
GB—Boyd Dowler 18 pass from Bart Starr (Jerry Kramer kick)

FOURTH QUARTER
MIN—Jerry Reichow 6 pass from Fran Tarkenton (Jim Christopherson kick)
MIN—Mel Triplett 1 run (Jim Christopherson kick)
GB—Tom Moore 6 run (Jerry Kramer kick)
GB—Elijah Pitts 7 run (Jerry Kramer kick)

INDIVIDUAL STATS

Passing GB—Bart Starr 20–28–297–3–0; John Roach 0–1–0–0–0. MIN—Fran Tarkenton 18–29–288–2–3.

Rushing GB—Jim Taylor 17–164; Bart Starr 3–6; Tom Moore 13–17–1; Paul Hornung 6–10–1; Elijah Pitts 2–9–1; Earl Gros 1–3. MIN—Fran Tarkenton 2–8; Hugh McElhenny 5–9; Doug Mayberry 5–18; Mel Triplett 4–8–1; Tommy Mason 3–3.

Receiving GB—Jim Taylor 1–(–1); Max McGee 10–159–2; Boyd Dowler 7–124–1; Paul Hornung 1–3; Ron Kramer 1–12. MIN—Hugh McElhenny 5–118; Charley Ferguson 4–84; Jerry Reichow 6–52–1; Doug Mayberry 1–11; Steve Stonebreaker 1–19–1; Tommy Mason 1–4.

GAME 6:
Green Bay 31, San Francisco 13

TEAM STATS

	SF	GB
First downs	14	19
Rush-yards-TDs	36–163–0	34–251–3
Comp-Att-Yd-TD-INT	6–15–41–0–3	10–12–107–1–0
Sacked-yards	2–22	2–22
Net pass yards	19	85
Total yards	182	336
Fumbles-lost	0–0	1–0
Turnovers	3	0
Penalties-yards	3–26	2–55

	1	2	3	4	FINAL
SAN FRANCISCO 49ERS (3–3)	3	3	7	0	13
GREEN BAY PACKERS (6–0)	0	10	14	7	31

SCORING

FIRST QUARTER

SF—Tommy Davis 31 field goal

SECOND QUARTER

SF—Tommy Davis 13 field goal
GB—Tom Moore 14 run (Jerry Kramer kick)
GB—Jerry Kramer 27 field goal

THIRD QUARTER

SF—Abe Woodson 85 punt return (Tommy Davis kick)
GB—Jim Taylor 16 run (Jerry Kramer kick)
GB—Jim Taylor 25 run (Jerry Kramer kick)

FOURTH QUARTER
GB—Ron Kramer 9 pass from Bart Starr (Jerry Kramer kick)

INDIVIDUAL STATS

Passing SF—John Brodie 6–15–41–0–3. GB—Bart Starr 10–12–107–1–0.

Rushing SF—J.D. Smith 26–119; John Brodie 1–16; Billy Kilmer 4–24; Bob Gaiters 4–6; Jim Vollenweider 1–(–2). GB—Jim Taylor 17–160–2; Tom Moore 14–84–1; Bart Starr 1–1; Elijah Pitts 1–8; Earl Gros 1–(–2).

Receiving SF—Billy Kilmer 1–6; Monty Stickles 2–21; Clyde Conner 1–8; Bernie Casey 2–6. GB—Jim Taylor 3–1; Ron Kramer 4–67–1; Boyd Dowler 2–34; Max McGee 1–5.

GAME 7:
Green Bay 17, Baltimore 6

TEAM STATS

	GB	BAL
First downs	14	18
Rush-yards-TDs	29–111–1	38–155–0
Comp-Att-Yd-TD-INT	11–19–152–1–2	18–31–161–0–2
Sacked-yards	1–11	1–7
Net pass yards	141	154
Total yards	252	309
Fumbles-lost	0–0	1–1
Turnovers	2	3
Penalties-yards	5–74	5–89

	1	2	3	4	FINAL
GREEN BAY PACKERS (7–0)	0	10	0	7	17
BALTIMORE COLTS (3–4)	0	3	3	0	6

SCORING

SECOND QUARTER
GB—Jerry Kramer 23 field goal
BAL—Dick Bielski 34 field goal
GB—Ron Kramer 25 pass from Bart Starr (Jerry Kramer kick)

THIRD QUARTER
BAL—Dick Bielski 34 field goal

FOURTH QUARTER
GB—Jim Taylor 37 run (Jerry Kramer kick)

INDIVIDUAL STATS

Passing GB—Bart Starr 11–19–152–1–2. BAL—Johnny Unitas 18–30–161–0–1; Lamar McHan 0–1–0–0–0.

Rushing GB—Bart Starr 1–18; Jim Taylor 16–68–1; Tom Moore 11–25; Elijah Pitts 1–0. BAL—Lenny Moore 18–77; Joe Perry 16–70; Johnny Unitas 2–1; Alex Hawkins 1–7; Tom Matte 1–0.

Receiving GB—Ron Kramer 3–76–1; Jim Taylor 2–(–4); Max McGee 3–51; Tom Moore 1–1; Lew Carpenter 1–22; Boyd Dowler 1–6. BAL—Lenny Moore 4–36; Joe Perry 4–22; Jimmy Orr 4–42; Raymond Berry 3–36; Dick Bielski 2–25; Mark Smolinski 1–0.

GAME 8:
Green Bay 38, Chicago 7

TEAM STATS

	GB	CHI
First downs	25	16
Rush-yards-TDs	44–215–5	27–65–0
Comp-Att-Yd-TD-INT	14–27–181–0–0	13–26–147–1–3
Sacked-yards	2–20	0–0

Net pass yards	161	147
Total yards	376	212
Fumbles-lost	0–0	7–4
Turnovers	0	7
Penalties-yards	6–78	3–25

	1	2	3	4	FINAL
GREEN BAY PACKERS (8–0)	7	3	7	21	38
CHICAGO BEARS (4–4)	7	0	0	0	7

SCORING

FIRST QUARTER
GB—Jim Taylor 2 run (Jerry Kramer kick)

SECOND QUARTER
CHI—John Adams 4 pass from Billy Wade (Roger LeClerc kick)
GB—Jerry Kramer 17 field goal

THIRD QUARTER
GB—Jim Taylor 1 run (Jerry Kramer kick)

FOURTH QUARTER
GB—Jim Taylor 1 run (Jerry Kramer kick)
GB—Jim Taylor 2 run (Jerry Kramer kick)
GB—Earl Gros 9 run (Jerry Kramer kick)

INDIVIDUAL STATS

Passing GB—Bart Starr 14–26–181–0–0; John Roach 0–1–0–0–0. CHI—Billy Wade 13–24–147–1–2; Rick Casares 0–1–0–0–0; Rudy Bukich 0–1–0–0–0.

Rushing GB—Jim Taylor 25–124–4; Tom Moore 12–38; Bart Starr 2–3; Earl Gros 3–40–1; Elijah Pitts 1–5; John Roach 1–5. CHI—Billy Wade 8–21; Rick Casares 5–14; Joe Marconi 4–29; Ronnie Bull 8–10; Johnny Morris 1–3; Charlie Bivins 1–(–12).

Receiving GB—Jim Taylor 2–8; Tom Moore 3–60; Max McGee 4–58; Lew Carpenter 3–33; Ron Kramer 2–22. CHI—Mike Ditka 5–79; Rick Casares 2–33; Joe Marconi 2–10; Ronnie Bull 2–9; Johnny Morris 1–12; John Adams 1–4–1.

GAME 9:
Green Bay 49, Philadelphia 0

TEAM STATS

	GB	PHI
First downs	37	3
Rush-yards-TDs	55–294–6	13–30–0
Comp-Att-Yd-TD-INT	19–31–334–1–1	9–25–56–0–1
Sacked-yards	0–0	4–32
Net pass yards	334	24
Total yards	628	54
Fumbles-lost	1–1	0–0
Turnovers	2	1
Penalties-yards	4–29	4–44

	1	2	3	4	FINAL
GREEN BAY PACKERS (9–0)	7	28	14	0	49
PHILADELPHIA EAGLES (1–7–1)	0	0	0	0	0

SCORING

FIRST QUARTER

GB—Tom Moore 3 run (Jerry Kramer kick)

SECOND QUARTER

GB—Jim Taylor 5 run (Jerry Kramer kick)
GB—Tom Moore 7 run (Jerry Kramer kick)
GB—Boyd Dowler 25 pass from Tom Moore (Jerry Kramer kick)
GB—Jim Taylor 1 run (Jerry Kramer kick)

THIRD QUARTER

GB—Jim Taylor 4 run (Jerry Kramer kick)
GB—Jim Taylor 5 run (Jerry Kramer kick)

INDIVIDUAL STATS

Passing GB—Bart Starr 15–20–274–0–1; Tom Moore 1–3–25–1–0; Paul Hornung 2–2–31–0–0; Elijah Pitts 0–1–0–0–0; John Roach 1–5–4–0–0. PHI—Sonny Jurgensen 4–13–35–0–1; King Hill 5–12–21–0–0.

Rushing GB—Max McGee 1–36; Jim Taylor 25–141–4; Bart Starr 2–12; Tom Moore 14–49–2; Earl Gros 7–39; Paul Hornung 1–4; Elijah Pitts 5–13. PHI—Clarence Peaks 7–27; Timmy Brown 6–3.

Receiving GB—Max McGee 7–174; Jim Taylor 1–22; Boyd Dowler 7–101–1; Ron Kramer 2–24; Elijah Pitts 1–4; Lew Carpenter 1–9. PHI—Clarence Peaks 4–29; Howard Cassady 2–13; Tommy McDonald 1–11; Bobby Walston 1–3; Timmy Brown 1–0.

GAME 10:
Green Bay 17, Baltimore 13

TEAM STATS

	BAL	GB
First downs	19	8
Rush-yards-TDs	44–189–0	27–87–1
Comp-Att-Yd-TD-INT	17–28–237–1–1	8–13–57–0–0
Sacked-yards	5–44	3–28
Net pass yards	193	29
Total yards	382	116
Fumbles-lost	3–2	4–2
Turnovers	3	2
Penalties-yards	5–76	1–5

	1	2	3	4	FINAL
BALTIMORE COLTS (5–5)	3	7	3	0	13
GREEN BAY PACKERS (10–0)	10	0	0	7	17

SCORING

FIRST QUARTER
BAL—Dick Bielski 42 field goal
GB—Herb Adderley 103 kickoff return (Jerry Kramer kick)
GB—Jerry Kramer 24 field goal

SECOND QUARTER
BAL—Jimmy Orr 34 pass from Johnny Unitas (Dick Bielski kick)

THIRD QUARTER
BAL—Dick Bielski 18 field goal

FOURTH QUARTER
GB—Tom Moore 23 run (Jerry Kramer kick)

INDIVIDUAL STATS

Passing BAL—Johnny Unitas 17–28–237–1–1. GB—Bart Starr 8–13–57–0–0.

Rushing BAL—Johnny Unitas 8–59; Lenny Moore 13–65; Mark Smolinski 17–41; Bobby Boyd 1–15; Tom Matte 3–8; Alex Hawkins 2–1. GB—Jim Taylor 19–46; Tom Moore 8–38–1; Bart Starr 1–3.

Receiving BAL—Jimmy Orr 5–100–1; R.C. Owens 6–84; Lenny Moore 3–11; Mark Smolinski 1–18; Dee Mackey 2–24. GB—Tom Moore 2–(–1); Max McGee 2–26; Boyd Dowler 2–17; Ron Kramer 2–15.

GAME 11:
Detroit 26, Green Bay 14

TEAM STATS

	GB	DET
First downs	11	14
Rush-yards-TDs	27–73–1	40–157–0
Comp-Att-Yd-TD-INT	11–19–142–0–2	10–18–147–2–2
Sacked-yards	10–93	0–0

	1	2	3	4	FINAL
Net pass yards	49				147
Total yards	122				304
Fumbles-lost	5–3				3–3
Turnovers	5				5
Penalties–yards	3–25				6–59

	1	2	3	4	FINAL
GREEN BAY PACKERS (10–1)	0	0	0	14	14
DETROIT LIONS (9–2)	7	16	3	0	26

SCORING

FIRST QUARTER

DET—Gail Cogdill 33 pass from Milt Plum (Wayne H. Walker kick)
DET—Gail Cogdill 27 pass from Milt Plum (Wayne H. Walker kick)

SECOND QUARTER

DET—Sam Williams 6 fumble return (Wayne H. Walker kick)
DET— Safety

THIRD QUARTER

DET— Milt Plum 47 field goal

FOURTH QUARTER

GB—Willie Davis 0 fumble return (Jerry Kramer kick)
GB—Jim Taylor 4 run (Jerry Kramer kick)

INDIVIDUAL STATS

Passing GB—Bart Starr 11–19–142–0–2. DET—Milt Plum 8–16–137–2–2; Earl Morrall 2–2–10–0–0.

Rushing GB—Bart Starr 4–(–6); Jim Taylor 13–47–1; Max McGee 1–8; Tom Moore 9–24. DET—Milt Plum 1–12; Ken Webb 11–62; Tom Watkins 17–55; Dan Lewis 7–16; Earl Morrall 3–9; Nick Pietrosante 1–3.

Receiving GB—Ron Kramer 4–62; Max McGee 2–37; Boyd Dowler 4–41; Tom Moore 1–2. DET—Gail Cogdill 3–79–2; Ken Webb 1–2; Tom Watkins 1–7; Pat Studstill 2–35; Jim Gibbons 3–25.

GAME 12:
Green Bay 41, Los Angeles 10

TEAM STATS

	LA	GB
First downs	14	24
Rush-yards-TDs	29–146–1	34–146–3
Comp-Att-Yd-TD-INT	18–28–139–0–1	16–24–278–2–1
Sacked-yards	5–48	7–60
Net pass yards	91	218
Total yards	237	364
Fumbles-lost	3–2	2–1
Turnovers	3	2
Penalties-yards	8–67	4–43

	1	2	3	4	FINAL
Los Angeles Rams (1–10–1)	3	0	0	7	10
Green Bay Packers (11–1)	10	14	3	14	41

SCORING

FIRST QUARTER

GB-Paul Hornung 30 pass from Bart Starr (Jerry Kramer kick)
LA—Danny Villanueva 13 field goal
GB—Jerry Kramer 35 field goal

SECOND QUARTER

GB—Jim Taylor 1 run (Jerry Kramer kick)
GB—Ron Kramer 4 pass from Bart Starr (Jerry Kramer kick)

THIRD QUARTER

GB—Jerry Kramer 37 field goal

FOURTH QUARTER

GB—Jim Taylor 2 run (Jerry Kramer kick)
LA—Dick Bass 5 run (Danny Villanueva kick)
GB—Earl Gros 15 run (Jerry Kramer kick)

INDIVIDUAL STATS

Passing LAR—Roman Gabriel 18–26–139–0–1; Dick Bass 0–2–0–0–0. GB—Bart Starr 15–20–260–2–0; Paul Hornung 0–1–0–0–0; John Roach 1–2–18–0–0; Elijah Pitts 0–1–0–0–0.

Rushing LAR—Roman Gabriel 4–36; Dick Bass 14–90–1; Art Perkins 4–11; Glenn Shaw 7–9. GB—Bart Starr 1–(–1); Paul Hornung 9–27; Jim Taylor 16–71–2; Earl Gros 5–45–1; Elijah Pitts 2–3; Tom Moore 1–1.

Receiving LAR—Dick Bass 4–13; Red Phillips 5–50; Art Perkins 4–23; Pervis Atkins 3–32; Glenn Shaw 2–21. GB—Paul Hornung 2–65–1; Jim Taylor 1–7; Max McGee 4–67; Boyd Dowler 4–67; Lew Carpenter 2–40; Ron Kramer 3–32–1.

GAME 13:
Green Bay 31, San Francisco 21

TEAM STATS

	GB	SF
First downs	20	18
Rush-yards-TDs	43–164–3	20–36–1
Comp-Att-Yd-TD-INT	10–18–130–1–1	20–31–269–2–2
Sacked-yards	0–0	0–0
Net pass yards	130	269
Total yards	294	305
Fumbles-lost	2–0	2–1
Turnovers	1	3
Penalties-yards	3–14	5–64

	1	**2**	**3**	**4**	**FINAL**
GREEN BAY PACKERS (12–1)	3	7	7	14	31
SAN FRANCISCO 49ERS (6–7)	7	14	0	0	21

SCORING

FIRST QUARTER

SF—J.D. Smith 1 run (Tommy Davis kick)
GB—Jerry Kramer 17 field goal

SECOND QUARTER

SF—Monty Stickles 3 pass from John Brodie (Tommy Davis kick)
GB—Tom Moore 5 run (Jerry Kramer kick)
SF—Clyde Conner 5 pass from John Brodie (Tommy Davis kick)

THIRD QUARTER

GB—Tom Moore 32 run (Jerry Kramer kick)

FOURTH QUARTER

GB—Jim Taylor 2 run (Jerry Kramer kick)
GB—Ron Kramer 8 pass from Bart Starr (Jerry Kramer kick)

INDIVIDUAL STATS

Passing GB—Bart Starr 10–18–130–1–1. SF – John Brodie 20–31–269–2–2.

Rushing GB—Jim Taylor 24–79–1; Bart Starr 1–5; Tom Moore 13–56–2; Max McGee 1–8; Paul Hornung 4–16. SF—John Brodie 2–10; J.D. Smith 13–18–1; Bob Gaiters 4–5; Jim Vollenweider 1–3.

Receiving GB—Jim Taylor 1–1; Ron Kramer 4–48–1; Boyd Dowler 4–47; Max McGee 1–34. SF—Bernie Casey 7–134; Jimmy Johnson 3–50; Clyde Conner 4–44–1; Monty Stickles 3–32–1; J.D. Smith 3–9.

GAME 14:
Green Bay 20, Los Angeles 17

TEAM STATS

	GB	LA
First downs	18	16
Rush-yards-TDs	33–181–1	36–207–0
Comp-Att-Yd-TD-INT	17–35–250–2–1	12–22–104–1–0
Sacked-yards	14	1–8
Net pass yards	246	96
Total yards	427	303
Fumbles-lost	3–2	2–1
Turnovers	3	1
Penalties-yards	1–5	1–5

	1	2	3	4	FINAL
GREEN BAY PACKERS (13–1)	7	6	0	7	20
LOS ANGELES RAMS (1–12–1)	3	7	0	7	17

SCORING

FIRST QUARTER

GB—Ron Kramer 45 pass from Tom Moore (Jerry Kramer kick)
LA—Danny Villanueva 39 field goal

SECOND QUARTER

GB—Jim Taylor 28 run (kick failed)
LA—Merlin Olsen 20 interception return (Danny Villanueva kick)

FOURTH QUARTER

GB—Paul Hornung 83 pass from Bart Starr (Jerry Kramer kick)
LA—Carroll Dale 15 pass from Jon Arnett (Danny Villanueva kick)

INDIVIDUAL STATS

Passing GB—Bart Starr 16–32–205–1–0; Max McGee 0–1–0–0–1; Tom Moore 1–1–45–1–0; John Roach 0–1–0–0–0. LAR—Roman Gabriel 10–20–80–0–0; Jon Arnett 2–2–24–1–0.

Rushing GB—Jim Taylor 23–156–1; Bart Starr 1–2; Paul Hornung 4–10; Tom Moore 5–13. LAR—Jon Arnett 16–103; Dick Bass 16–78; Roman Gabriel 4–76.

Receiving GB—Jim Taylor 3–8; Paul Hornung 2–88–1; Ron Kramer 4–73–1; Max McGee 5–58; Tom Moore 1–15; Boyd Dowler 2–8. LAR—Jon Arnett 1–(–6); Dick Bass 3–9; Carroll Dale 4–64–1; Red Phillips 3–30; Pervis Atkins 1–7.

GAME 15:
Green Bay 16, New York Giants 7

TEAM STATS

	GB	NYG
First downs	18	18
Rush-yards-TDs	46–148–1	26–94–0
Comp-Att-Yd-TD-INT	10–22–106–0–0	18–41–197–0–1
Sacked-yards	1–10	0–0
Net pass yards	96	197
Total yards	244	291
Fumbles-lost	2–0	3–2
Turnovers	0	3
Penalties-yards	5–44	4–62

	1	2	3	4	FINAL
GREEN BAY PACKERS (14–1)	3	7	3	3	16
NEW YORK GIANTS (12–3)	0	0	7	0	7

SCORING

FIRST QUARTER

GB—Jerry Kramer 26 field goal

SECOND QUARTER

GB—Jim Taylor 7 run (Jerry Kramer kick)

THIRD QUARTER

NYG—Jim Collier 0 fumble return (Don Chandler kick)
GB—Jerry Kramer 29 field goal

FOURTH QUARTER

GB—Jerry Kramer 30 field goal

INDIVIDUAL STATS

Passing GB—Bart Starr 9–21–85–0–0; Paul Hornung 1–1–21–0–0. NYG—Y.A. Tittle 18–41–197–0–1.

Rushing GB—Jim Taylor 31–85–1; Bart Starr 1–4; Paul Hornung 8–35; Tom Moore 6–24. NYG—Alex Webster 15–56; Phil King 11–38.

Receiving GB—Jim Taylor 3–20; Boyd Dowler 4–48; Ron Kramer 2–25; Max McGee 1–13. NYG—Joe Walton 5–75; Del Shofner 5–69; Alex Webster 1–6; Phil King 2–14; Frank Gifford 4–34; Joe Morrison 1–0.

Roster

No. 26 DB Herb Adderley

No. 80 WR Gary Barnes

No. 60 G Ed Blaine

No. 33 RB/E Lew Carpenter

No. 58 LB Dan Currie

No. 87 DE/T Willie Davis

No. 86 WR/DE Boyd Dowler

No. 71 LB/DT Bill Forester

No. 73 DT Ron Gassert

No. 75 T Forrest Gregg

No. 46 DB Hank Gremminger

No. 40 RB Earl Gros

No. 79 DT Dave Hanner

No. 5 RB Paul Hornung

No. 53 C Ken Iman

No. 78 DT/DE * Henry Jordan

No. 84 E Gary Knafelc

No. 77 DT Ron Kostelnik

No. 64 G Jerry Kramer

No. 88 TE Ron Kramer

No. 78 T Norm Masters

No. 85 E Max McGee

No. 25 RB Tom Moore

No. 66 LB Ray Nitschke

No. 22 RB Elijah Pitts

No. 83 DE Bill Quinlan

No. 51 C Jim Ringo

No. 10 QB John Roach

No. 78 Bob Skoronski

No. 15 Bart Starr

No. 27 DB Johnny Symank

No. 31 FB Jim Taylor

No. 63 G Fuzzy Thurston

No. 61 LB Nelson Toburen

No. 47 DB Jesse Whittenton

No. 29 DB Howie Williams

No. 24 S Willie Wood

1962 NFL standings

	W	L	T	PCT	PF	PA
EAST						
New York Giants	12	2	0	.857	398	283
Pittsburgh Steelers	9	5	0	.643	312	363
Cleveland Browns	7	6	1	.538	291	257
Washington Redskins	5	7	2	.417	305	376
Dallas Cowboys	5	8	1	.385	398	402
St. Louis Cardinals	4	9	1	.308	287	361
Philadelphia Eagles	3	10	1	.231	282	356
WEST						
Green Bay Packers	13	1	0	.929	415	148
Detroit Lions	11	3	0	.786	315	177
Chicago Bears	9	5	0	.643	321	287
Baltimore Colts	7	7	0	.500	293	288
San Francisco 49ers	6	8	0	.429	282	331
Minnesota Vikings	2	11	1	.154	254	410
Los Angeles Rams	1	12	1	.077	220	334

TEAM OFFENSE

	G	PTS	YDS	CMP	PASSING ATT	PASSING YDS	TD	INT	RUSHING ATT	RUSHING YDS	TD
GREEN BAY PACKERS	14	415	4791	187	311	2331	14	13	518	2460	36
NEW YORK GIANTS	14	398	5005	215	411	3307	35	22	430	1698	11
DALLAS COWBOYS	14	398	4912	200	380	2872	31	17	434	2040	16
CHICAGO BEARS	14	321	4549	229	430	3060	20	28	356	1489	17
DETROIT LIONS	14	315	4503	211	379	2581	19	24	489	1922	14
PITTSBURGH STEELERS	14	312	4402	160	319	2069	14	23	572	2333	17
WASHINGTON REDSKINS	14	305	4311	223	428	3223	27	27	371	1088	10
BALTIMORE COLTS	14	293	4666	237	423	3065	27	25	448	1601	9
CLEVELAND BROWNS	14	291	4306	200	370	2534	17	16	414	1772	18
ST. LOUIS CARDINALS	14	287	4798	220	434	3100	18	30	416	1698	20
PHILADELPHIA EAGLES	14	282	4540	228	428	3385	23	31	324	1155	13
SAN FRANCISCO 49ERS	14	282	3941	185	323	2068	19	19	460	1873	15
MINNESOTA VIKINGS	14	254	4080	170	348	2216	22	31	426	1864	7
LOS ANGELES RAMS	14	220	3865	189	372	2176	14	19	376	1689	10

TEAM DEFENSE

	G	PTS	YDS	CMP	PASSING ATT	YDS	TD	INT	RUSHING ATT	YDS	TD
GREEN BAY PACKERS	14	148	3277	187	355	1746	10	31	404	1531	4
DETROIT LIONS	14	177	3217	187	367	1986	11	24	353	1231	6
CLEVELAND BROWNS	14	257	3924	189	341	1984	15	24	466	1940	17
NEW YORK GIANTS	14	283	4546	223	450	2869	21	26	413	1677	13
CHICAGO BEARS	14	287	4147	170	363	2074	14	23	438	2073	17
BALTIMORE COLTS	14	288	4123	206	381	2619	19	23	423	1504	17
SAN FRANCISCO 49ERS	14	331	4549	164	296	2308	17	12	464	2241	22
LOS ANGELES RAMS	14	334	4981	217	379	2889	25	19	501	2092	14
PHILADELPHIA EAGLES	14	356	5046	198	363	2920	16	26	526	2126	23
ST. LOUIS CARDINALS	14	361	4711	196	377	2987	21	16	452	1724	18
PITTSBURGH STEELERS	14	363	4625	223	438	3206	34	28	363	1419	13
WASHINGTON REDSKINS	14	376	5238	247	412	3602	35	28	411	1636	12
DALLAS COWBOYS	14	402	5184	233	437	3674	33	20	387	1510	17
MINNESOTA VIKINGS	14	410	5101	214	397	3123	29	25	463	1978	20

Bibliography

Most of the materials used in this book came from newspaper accounts of the 1962 season. Papers used included the *Green Bay Press–Gazette*; *Milwaukee Journal*; and *Milwaukee Sentinel*. Green Bay Packers GameDay programs from the 2009 season also were used.

The following books were also used as resources:

That First Season, How Vince Lombardi Took the Worst Team in the NFL and Set It on a Path to Glory, by John Eisenberg. Mariner Books, 2009.

When Pride Still Mattered: A Life of Vince Lombardi, by David Maraness. New York: Simon & Schuster, 1999.

Lombardi and Me: Players, Coaches, and Colleagues Talk About the Man and the Myth, by Paul Hornung with Billy Reed. Triumph Books, 2004.

Giants: What I Learned from Vince Lombardi and Tom Landry, by Pat Summerall with Michael Levin. Wiley & Sons, 2010.

Bart Starr: When Leadership Mattered, by David Claerbaut. Taylor Trade Publishing, 2004.

Launching the Glory Years: The 1959 Packers, by Len Wagner. Published by Jay Bengtson.

Mudbaths and Bloodbaths: The Inside Story on the Bears–Packers Rivalry, by Gary D'Amato and Cliff Christl. Prairie Oak Press.

Nitschke, by Edward Gruver. Taylor Trade Publishing, 2002.

Acknowledgments

First and foremost I'd like to thank everyone who was interviewed for this book, the Packer players from 1962 and those who played against them. Your stories were fascinating, and you took me back to 1962 when Sunday afternoons were spent with my father and brothers watching No. 15 throw touchdown passes to Nos. 85, 86, and 88; Nos. 5 and 31 run for touchdowns behind the guys wearing Nos. 63 and 64; Nos. 78 and 87 smother opposing quarterbacks; No. 66 knocking down everyone in his path; and Nos. 24 and 26 making countless interceptions.

I would like to thank Mary Jane Herber of the Brown County Library in Green Bay for helping provide materials for this book, and Jason McGill, who typed in the game summaries. Also, thanks to the *Green Bay Press–Gazette* for the photos in this book, and to Jeff Ash, who helped select the photos.

Special thanks to my good friend Charles (Whip) Wiener, one of the biggest Packer fans I know. He spent several days helping me research newspaper accounts of the 1962 season. It was fun not only to relive these games but also events that occurred in 1962; Mercury spaceflights; Marilyn Monroe's death; Wisconsin's march to the Rose Bowl; the Cuban Missile Crisis. Research can be a tedious task, but Whip made the days fly by, and his observations helped give me a clear vision for this book.

I'd also like to thank the good folks at Clerisy Press for teaming up with me on another football book.

Last and certainly not least, I can't express how thrilled I am to have Bart Starr, the quarterback of the 1962 Packers and of their four other championships during the Lombardi era, write the foreword to this book. His name gives this account of that special season credibility, and I'll forever be indebted to one of the classiest Hall of Famers of all time.

INDEX

About the Author

BOB BERGHAUS was born in 1954 and raised in Milwaukee. He went on to work for the *Milwaukee Journal* and *Milwaukee Journal Sentinel* where he reported on a variety of sports, including the Milwaukee Brewers from 1991–95 and the Green Bay Packers from 1996–98, covering the Packers in Super Bowls XXXI and XXXII. He then moved to Green Bay to become sports editor of the *Green Bay Press-Gazette*. He's earned several writing awards and was named Wisconsin Sportswriter of the Year in 1991 by the National Sportscasters and Sportswriters Association. Bob left Green Bay in the summer of 2003 for Asheville, North Carolina, where he is currently sports editor of the *Asheville Citizen-Times*. He and his wife, Lisa, have a daughter, Kelly.